Writing in the Time
of Nationalism

D0760745

Writing in the Time of Nationalism

From Two Solitudes
to Blue Metropolis

Linda Leith

Signature
EDITIONS

Cover design by Relish Design.
Photo of Author by Judith Lermer Crawley.

Acknowledgements
I would like to thank Ann Charney, Patrick Coleman, Anne Lagacé Dowson, Rita Legault, Annabelle Moreau, Lorraine O'Donnell, and Karen Haughian for their comments and insights.

This book was printed on Ancient Forest Friendly paper.
Printed and bound in Canada by Marquis Book Printing Inc.

We acknowledge the support of the Canada Council for the Arts and the Manitoba Arts Council for our publishing program.

Library and Archives Canada Cataloguing in Publication

Leith, Linda
 Writing in the time of nationalism : from Two Solitudes to Blue Metropolis / Linda Leith.

Includes bibliographical references and index.
ISBN 978-1-897109-48-9

 1. Canadian literature--20th century--History and criticism.
2. Nationalism and literature--Canada--History--20th century.
3. Authors, Canadian--20th century--Biography. I. Title.

PS8061.L44 2010 C810.9'0054 C2010-906215-9

Signature Editions
P.O. Box 206, RPO Corydon, Winnipeg, Manitoba, R3M 3S7
www.signature-editions.com

To my teachers

Contents

This overlapping in one room of French and English, of Catholic and Protestant — my parents' way of being, and so to me life itself — was as unlikely, as unnatural to the Montreal climate as a school of tropical fish. Only later would I discover that most other people simply floated in mossy little ponds labeled "French and Catholic" or "English and Protestant," never wondering what it might be like to step ashore; or wondering, perhaps, but weighing up the danger. To be out of a pond is to be in unmapped territory. The earth might be flat; you could fall over the edge quite easily.

— Mavis Gallant

If there is dissatisfaction with the status quo, good. If there is ferment, so much the better. If there is restlessness, I am pleased. Then let there be ideas, and hard thought, and hard work.

—Hubert M. Humphrey

1
Separate Legends

The story I have to tell begins in the glory days when Hugh MacLennan published *Two Solitudes* in 1945 and Mavis Gallant, Brian Moore, and Mordecai Richler emerged on to the international literary scene in the 1950s. It's a story that moves into a long decline in English-language Montreal fiction that started in the 1960s, when nationalism was on the rise, and lasted more than three decades. This is a literary story, in other words, and a literary story best understood in the context of the time.

It's a personal story, as well. I am not from Montreal, but I am more at home here than anywhere else, having lived here for most of the time since immigrating with my family in 1963. I became interested in Quebec, and sympathized with Quebec's frustrations and aspirations. When I started teaching and writing about the work of Montreal writers in the late 1970s and 1980s, I focused on writers working in French as well as in English, and I discovered that Montreal's English-language writers had now disappeared from sight. I got involved in working to create the context in which it would be possible for them to thrive. I myself became a writer, and when I got to know other writers, a couple of us crossed town to work with French-speaking writers. By the late 1990s, I was part of a small group convinced that Montreal needed an international literary festival that would bring together writers working in English and French and other languages. I called it Blue Metropolis.

The story I have to tell continues to evolve, as new writers, new books, and new events appear on the scene every season. It's a story worth telling, for it has a good shape, with a glorious beginning, a disheartening middle, and a better ending than any of us could have predicted. The Anglo Literary Revival is what we were working for all along, even if we never imagined it would happen.

The divisions between Canada and Quebec provide the context. Canada and Quebec have much in common, including a shared history, but even our shared history divides us, for it is viewed one way in Canada and quite differently in Quebec. The differences between us have led us to the brink of separation twice in recent memory, when the population of Quebec voted whether or not to begin the process of seceding from Canada to form an independent Quebec.

The federalists won the first Referendum, in 1980, with some 60 per cent of the vote; 40 per cent of Quebecers voted instead for sovereignty-association. The second Referendum was in 1995, when there was a real possibility that a majority of Quebecers might vote to split up the country. The extent of the danger became clear only late in the day. Federal Minister Brian Tobin — dubbed "Captain Canada" — marshalled together thousands of Canadians from outside of Quebec and bused them into Montreal for a pro-Canada rally on October 27, 1995. Canadians thought the "My Canada includes Quebec" rally a friendly gesture to show Quebecers how much they wanted Quebec to stay in Canada. Quebecers saw the influx of federalists differently. The *Journal de Montréal* described the unity rally as an "invasion by English Canada," and polls showed support for the federalist side actually dropped after the rally (Fraser 2006, 288). When the votes were cast, the country had survived, but only barely, with a narrow majority of 50.58 per cent of the vote.

It was a referendum that would leave an unhappy legacy. Federalists complained that ballot boxes had been rigged and votes destroyed; *indépendantistes*, for their part, were angered by the expenditure of federal funds on national unity. Editorial writers in Montreal lamented division and cast about for signs of *rapprochement*.

One of the most influential of the editorialists was Lise Bissonnette, publisher of *Le Devoir*, who found that some of Montreal's English-speaking musicians and performing artists, writers, and

translators were looking to bridge the divides. In galleries, museums, and cafés, she wrote in February 1996, there were Anglo artists who "feel close to Quebec as it is, and especially as it could be if they had a bigger role to play" (Bissonnette 1996).

I was one of the readers Bissonnette spoke to. I was also one of the writers she was speaking about. In 1996, I was on the executive of the Writers' Union of Canada, and was involved in planning an event that would bring the city's English and French writers together in a historic collaboration with the French-language Union des écrivaines et des écrivains québécois. The event, which was called Write pour écrire, took place on October 31st, 1996 and showed that there was an audience in Montreal for a literary event that included both French and English. I did not know at the time that the Blue Metropolis Montreal International Literary Festival would eventually come of this, but it did.

The literary world was improbable ground for bridge building, for writing and publishing are language-based. Most Montreal writing and publishing takes place in French, and the city's French-language writers were living in a world that had little in common with the much smaller world of the city's English-language writers — and little in common with Canadian literature, which is so often understood as being written in English.

When you're talking about books, in fact, Canada does not often include Quebec. When it does, Quebec has a small or token presence. One of the issues on which we Canadians and *Québécois* are most likely to agree is that Canadian writing is in English and Quebec writing is in French.

People in the book trade — the writers themselves, the organizations that represent them, publishers, booksellers, librarians, reviewers — frequently talk about Canadian writers as though there were no writers in French.[1] University courses in Canadian literature are commonly housed in Departments of English and include few if any books in French or even in translation from French. "Canadian Studies" institutes and schools within Canada tend to offer courses in English for English-Canadian writers and courses in French for Quebec writers. "Quebec literature" has typically meant writing in French. University courses in Quebec literature focus on work written in French and seldom include books written in English.

Margaret Atwood is a Canadian writer; Michel Tremblay is a Quebec writer. When Atwood publishes a new book, it can be found in Canadian bookstores with other books written in English, whereas Tremblay's new book will be found in a different section with other books written in French. If and when his book is translated into English, it will appear with other English titles, just as the French translation of the Atwood novel will then appear with other books in French, but that will not change the fact that Atwood is a Canadian writer and Tremblay a Quebec writer.

For most practical purposes, Canada and Quebec have in literary terms been separated for decades. Somehow, when no one was looking, they became two different countries, with different languages and different literatures. No one denies this, and no harm is meant by this kind of shorthand. It isn't even controversial, so long as we're talking about books.

Politics is a different matter. For those of us who lived through the bitterness of the 1995 Referendum, the suggestion that Canada and Quebec are — or might ever be, or might never be — separate political entities is dangerous ground. The words we choose to use here are telling. Just talking about "Canada and Quebec" rather than just "Canada" is controversial, for "Canada and Quebec" gives Quebec status equal to that of Canada, which makes some federalists uneasy. It is similarly controversial to talk about "Canada" when you really mean "Canada outside of Quebec." In some contexts, that can offend French-speaking Quebecers who see Quebec as a "nation." English-speaking Quebecers are typically federalist, but there are contexts in which they, too, take exception at being lumped in with the Rest of Canada. There are real differences between Quebec and English Canada.

One of the most obvious of these differences involves bilingualism. Canada has two official languages, and bilingualism is federal policy, so that provides one kind of context for a discussion of the merits of bilingualism among English-speaking Canadians in Toronto, say. French being the only official language in Quebec, French-speaking Quebecers who support laws protecting the French language are uneasy about bilingualism, and English-speaking Montrealers view bilingualism very differently from our English-speaking Torontonian friends, as well.

Touting the virtues of bilingualism does not mean the same thing to us as it does to an English-Canadian living outside of Quebec. We are far more likely to be bilingual, for a start, and bilingualism is a necessity for many of us in our daily lives. In this we have more in common with Francophones living outside of Quebec than with most English-speaking Torontonians. French is not seen as any threat to English in Toronto, though, whereas there are good historical reasons why English is seen as a threat to the majority French-speaking population of Quebec and its language. Bilingualism simply does not apply in Quebec in the same way as it does outside of Quebec.

This is why we need locutions like "Canada outside of Quebec," "the Rest of Canada," "ROC," "English Canada," and "English-speaking Quebec." There are many subtleties, all of them requiring different locutions, and these locutions all have various shades of political meaning. There are opportunities to offend on both sides — all sides — of the political divide. If the merest whisper of separation may be sacrilege to an ardent Canadian, the idea of bilingualism may be anathema to a Quebec sovereignist.

This book is focused on Montreal, which is the city where our two languages and literatures meet and — as Hugh MacLennan wrote of the two races and religions of Canada — "live their separate legends side by side."

The line is from *Two Solitudes*, a novel in which Canada very much includes Quebec. MacLennan's novel is largely unread now, although its title has entered the language — the two languages — as an evocation of the gulf that separates the French and English of Canada. This is sadly ironic, for the quotation from Rilke that provides the title and the epigraph to the novel focuses not on separation but on coming together: "Love consists in this, that two solitudes protect and touch and greet each other."

Two Solitudes is worth rereading for what it tells us about how much has changed since it was published in 1945 — and how much remains the same. The novel begins with a foreword, in which MacLennan comments,

> Because this is a story, I dislike having to burden it with a foreword, but something of the kind is necessary, for it is a

novel of Canada. This means that its scene is laid in a nation with two official languages, English and French.

The first chapter opens with a description of how the Ottawa River flows out of Protestant Ontario into Catholic Quebec, where it joins the St. Lawrence and the "two streams embrace the pan of Montreal Island" before "the Ottawa merges and loses itself, and the mainstream moves northeastward a thousand miles to the sea."

This is a measured and confident voice, and the narrator is omniscient as he closes in on the narrow plain between the St. Lawrence and the hills, where the ploughed land "looks like the course of a gigantic and empty steeplechase where all motion has been frozen." You can look north across the plain and see the farms and beyond them the line of trees "crawling shaggily up the slope of the hills." Beyond this the evergreen bush spreads far to the north until it reaches the tundra.

> Winters make it a universe of snow with a terrible wind keening over it, and beyond its horizon the northern lights flare into walls of shifting electric colours that crack and roar like the gods of a dead planet talking to each other out of the dark.

There is no one with a voice like this. MacLennan is old-fashioned in his characterization, in his diction, in his phrasing, in his views of women and of Quebec and in any number of other ways. Stylistically he is especially old-fashioned in this powerful opening chapter to his most famous novel. MacLennan's fiction served him well in the 1940s and 1950s and into the 1960s, when he was the most celebrated Canadian writer of his day.

By 1967, however, a new wind was blowing through Canadian literature, and the old-fashioned qualities of MacLennan's fiction no longer sat well with Canadian reviewers. When his penultimate novel *Return of the Sphinx* appeared in 1967, Canadian reviewers treated him like yesterday's man.[2]

Reviewers of *Return of the Sphinx* were reflecting the taste and mores of their day, as reviewers do. Canadian literature and Canadian criticism have moved on in the intervening decades, and we are now in a position to reassess some of the great writers of the past. A literature needs a sense of where it comes from, and there is something to be

gained from acknowledging that MacLennan is one of the giants on whose shoulders we are standing.

It's unlikely that any writer today would choose to write like MacLennan, even if he were capable of doing so. We may or may not be aware of the ways in which MacLennan laid out some of the groundwork for writing about Canada in *Barometer Rising, Two Solitudes*, and *The Watch That Ends the Night*. We might find we have underestimated the extent to which he opened a door that Mavis Gallant and Margaret Atwood and younger writers were able to walk through.

The opening chapter of *Two Solitudes* focuses in on Montreal, "the island about which the two rivers join":

> Two old races and religions meet here and live their separate legends, side by side. If this sprawling half-continent has a heart, here it is. Its pulse throbs out along the rivers and railroads; slow, reluctant and rarely simple, a double beat, a self-moved reciprocation.

Most French-speaking Montrealers were Catholic, but not all English-speaking Montrealers were Protestant, for there were substantial Irish Catholic and Jewish populations as well as other minorities. MacLennan was well aware of this; his hero Paul Tallard's English-speaking mother is an Irish Catholic. There were always more than two solitudes in Montreal — people from other faiths, other races, and other countries — and the population has become far more diverse since MacLennan's day.[3]

There are still two great streams, though, and they still inspire a fervour that is religious in its intensity. No longer identifiable as Protestant and Catholic, as in MacLennan's novel, today these are the streams of rival nationalisms that speak different languages and express themselves in different literatures. The mingling between these languages and literatures has increased in recent years but, in some ways, they still live their separate legends, side by side.

The French language and literature is far more assertive in Montreal today than it was in 1945. The English language is seen and heard far less today than it was in the postwar years. Writers working here in English were soon reduced to the status of a small

and marginal literary community. MacLennan was far from the only writer whose work was poorly received in a long period of decline that lasted from the 1960s until the end of the century.

What is remarkable, though, is that the past dozen years have seen a literary revival among fiction writers working in English in Montreal.[4] Writers following in MacLennan's footsteps today are making their mark internationally to an extent rarely seen since his own heyday. This is a story of individual successes, of course, for literary success is always the success of an individual, and the stars of this revival have rightly had a great deal of attention, sometimes in the pages of the very same issue of the *New York Times Book Review*.

The success of an individual writer is not only the success of an individual, however. It rests on people who may live far away — an agent, a publisher, and critics, not to mention readers — and it rests on the literary context within which he works. As writers working in English in Montreal, the writers who have been making their mark in recent years have something in common with one another and with others whose careers have not — or not yet — known such success.

We writers differ from one another in countless ways. We may read one another's work with care, or not. We may see ourselves as members of a community, or not. We may covet success, or not. We may or may not agree on what success means. We may have been in Montreal for decades or for only a short time, as was true of the writers of the 1940s and 1950s as well. Those of us who have been here for long enough may — or may not — be aware of how Montreal's marginalized English-language literary community pulled itself back from the brink and created the conditions within which writers could thrive. The story I have to tell is the story of how this came about.

2
Writers Without a Country

In Hugh MacLennan's day, Montreal was the heart of Canada. It was the literary capital of Canada and the cradle of contemporary Canadian literature both in English and in French, not to mention Yiddish.

For English-Canadians, Canada means the nation, from sea to sea to sea: from the Atlantic all the way across to the Pacific and — in our imaginations, at least, since there are few of us who have ever been there — right up to the Arctic Sea. Sometimes that's what it means for us here in Quebec, too. In his foreword to *Two Solitudes*, Hugh MacLennan wrote:

> No single word exists, within Canada itself, to designate with satisfaction to both races a native of the country. When those of the French language use the word *Canadien*, they nearly always refer to themselves. They know their English-speaking compatriots as *les Anglais*. English-speaking citizens act on the same principle. They call themselves Canadians; those of the French language French-Canadians.

English- and French-speaking Canadians used different words for the other in the 1940s, but they used the same word to describe themselves to themselves: *Canadian / Canadien*.

This has changed. English Canadians still think of themselves as Canadians, plain and simple, but the man who lives in Quebec and

speaks French is less likely today to think of himself as a *Canadien*; he may see himself as a *Québécois*. English-Canadians have followed his lead: they, too, may call him a Quebecer or *Québécois*. He might still think of Canadians who speak English as *les Anglais*, but nowadays he's more likely to call English Canadians *Canadiens anglais* or simply *Canadiens*, depending on the context.[5] So English Canadians and Quebecers today agree to describe themselves using two *different* words: *Canadiens / Canadians* now generally means English-speaking Canadians; *Québécois* refers to people from Quebec.

We seem, in short, to have agreed to disagree. To the extent that there is a division between Canada and Quebec, this division is not only literary but linguistic: it has become intrinsic to the very words that many of us use to identify ourselves. We have also taken notice of the Quebec border; the million or so Francophones living outside Quebec are not *Québécois*; they are still "French-Canadians" (they are also Franco-Ontariens or Acadiens or Fransaskois). There are also some 600,000 of us living in Quebec whose mother tongue is English; this is the measure that Quebec uses to determine the size of the English-speaking community. We are over 900,000 members of the Official-language Minority, according to Statistics Canada.[6] Whatever the number, we are sometimes considered Québécois, and sometimes Québécois is reserved for Francophones.

MacLennan's Canada did include Quebec, and Montreal was the heart of the sprawling half-continent when he was writing *Two Solitudes*. Today, Montreal is the largest and most vibrant city in Quebec, but who now thinks of Montreal as the heart of Canada? We had no referendum on the language we use, but when no one was watching, we quietly agreed to use a language — languages — that suggest that Canada excludes Quebec.

We in Montreal all carry the same passport as Canadians from Toronto. We don't speak the same languages, though. I hear English, most of the time, on the streets of Toronto. When I hear other languages in Toronto, I hear Italian, Farsi, Chinese, any number of languages, but though there are many Francophones living in the Toronto area, I don't hear much French there. The only context there within which I have ever heard French, in fact, is at the Salon du livre de Toronto. In Montreal, I hear French most of the time, with a lot

of English in some parts of town and any one of a hundred other languages here and there in different neighbourhoods.

If Toronto sounds like a different country, it also looks like a different country, for we don't fly the same flag. The Maple Leaf of Canada is displayed proudly in Toronto. Here in Montreal, you seldom see the Maple Leaf except on federal buildings.

We're not all flag wavers, anyway, certainly not here in Quebec, where waving any flag is a provocation limited to blowouts like the June 24th holiday, Saint-Jean-Baptiste Day, an ancient religious holiday still celebrated in today's secular Quebec with bonfires and fireworks and now designated la Fête nationale du Québec. It's true that there's an annual show of *fleur de lys* on balconies and cars around here, not to mention a flutter of Italian flags on cars racing up The Main when Italy wins the World Cup — and of *Canadiens* pennants in playoff season. Aside from that, it's only in moments of national crisis that you'll see a lot of flags in Montreal.

The story of what has happened to Montreal fiction in English in the decades since the end of the Second World War is one of the most dramatic chapters in Canadian literary history.[7] This is a literary story, though some of it is personal, for I eventually came to play a role in how the story would unfold. Since its focus is Montreal, where language and literature are inevitably political, it is also a political story.

It begins in what author William Weintraub has called "the good old bad old days,"[8] when Maurice Duplessis ruled Quebec with an iron hand and Montreal was the literary capital of Canada. Some of the writers working here in English in those days did pretty well for themselves. There was Hugh MacLennan publishing his novels in New York — which was one measure of success — and winning awards for them. Constance Beresford-Howe and Joyce Marshall also had U.S. publishers. Gwethalyn Graham's *Earth and High Heaven* appeared in London and became a bestseller in the United States.

Mavis Gallant lived in Montreal as a child in the 1920s and then again in the 1940s before moving to Europe in 1950 and publishing short stories in *The New Yorker*. Mordecai Richler and Brian Moore made both a living and a literary reputation with internationally published novels in the 1950s and 1960s. The poets include not only

A.M. Klein, Frank Scott, Louis Dudek, and Irving Layton but also Leonard Cohen, who moved from poetry and experimental fiction to songwriting and became one of the great Canadian writers of his time.

Stephen Leacock, P.K. Page, A.J.M. Smith, Raymond Souster, John Glassco, Leon Edel, Leo Kennedy, Ralph Gustafson, and Chava Rosenfarb lived here, as did Adele Wiseman, Norman Levine, Margaret Laurence, Michael Ondaatje, George Bowering, and Margaret Atwood. There is hardly an English-Canadian writer of note who did not spend time here in Quebec and consider the pros and cons of living in an increasingly assertive French-speaking milieu. Montreal is a city with a formidable literary history, and the post-war years were its golden age.

I arrived in Montreal in 1963. I had been born in Belfast, where my family on both sides lived for generations on one of the ragged edges of the British Empire. My parents were anti-sectarian Communists, and we left Ireland for Beckenham, Kent, moved on to Basel, Switzerland, and then lived in London for three years before we crossed the Atlantic when I was 13 years old. I had no particular country, which may be one of the reasons I have found Montreal so congenial. Montreal has been a turbulent place to live, not only because of Quebec nationalism, but also because of the equal and opposite force of Canadian nationalism.

1963 was the year the nationalist Front de libération du Québec (FLQ) embarked on the violent campaign that culminated in 1970 with the kidnapping of the British High Commissioner James Cross, the murder of Quebec Minister of Labour Pierre Laporte, and the imposition of the War Measures Act by Prime Minister Pierre Elliott Trudeau. Quebec Premier Jean Lesage was, by 1963, halfway through his Quiet Revolution mandate of modernizing Quebec and establishing its control of its own destiny. His memorable campaign slogan was *Maîtres chez nous*, and he was in the process of instituting a series of far-reaching reforms and creating Hydro-Québec, the Caisse de dépôt et placement du Québec, and Ministries of Culture, Education, and Intergovernmental Affairs.

Quebec was not alone in its nationalist aspirations. Canada needed to carve out a distinct identity for itself and to safeguard its economy and its culture from British and American influence and

control. So Canada's new sense of itself was both cause and effect of the great debate over the adoption of the Maple Leaf flag to replace the Canadian Red Ensign in the mid-1960s. The cornerstones of what Canada has since become — universal health care, student loans, the Canada Pension Plan, the Order of Canada — were put in place in this period under Prime Minister Lester B. Pearson.[9]

There was lots of hand-wringing over the Canadian identity, but one thing was clear to most Canadians: whatever the Canadian identity was, it included French and English. And how much French? Not enough to please nationalist Québécois. For Quebec was asserting itself in opposition to Canada and the English language. The language of Quebec nationalism was French. The identity of Quebec was linked with the French language, especially after the importance of Catholicism waned.

Canada therefore needed Quebec in a way that Quebec did not need Canada. While Canadian nationalism was intent on claiming Quebec — and the French language — as a key to its identity, Quebec nationalism was intent on rejecting the English language — and Canada.

It was Pearson who, in 1963, convened the Royal Commission on Bilingualism and Biculturalism to study ways of preventing the country from splitting in two. By 1967, Canada's Centennial year, Quebec was taking its place on an international stage and inviting the world to Expo 67 in Montreal.

The literary effects of these rival nationalisms did not make the headlines, but they were dramatic, and Toronto soon emerged as the literary capital of Canada. Montreal was now the literary capital of Quebec. That left Montreal's English writers out in the cold.

For the literary history of English Montreal was very different from that of English Canada and different again from that of French Quebec. Though Montreal had been an exciting place to be a writer either in French or in English in the post-war years, nationalism had had a powerful effect. By the late 1960s, some of the most accomplished English writers had left Montreal for good, and those who stayed, as MacLennan did, saw their reputations go into a decline as steep as that of the English-speaking population.

It was at this time that I myself became part of the story. I had left Montreal in 1970 to study in Paris and London, then returned in 1974 to make Montreal my home. The writers who interested me most were the ones who had lived here in Montreal. I was interested in writing in French and reviewed Quebec books in the original French and in translation for *Quill & Quire* and *The Canadian Forum*. I was teaching English at John Abbott College, and in the early 1980s created a course on The Writers of English Montreal focused on the work of Hugh MacLennan and Mavis Gallant, Mordecai Richler, Brian Moore, and Leonard Cohen as well as some of the new generation of fiction writers.

I had written about Gallant, whose work I admired above all others, and in the mid-1980s embarked on a research project on Quebec's English writers in the course of which I interviewed many of the writers and wrote about their work. English Montreal had missed out on the massive growth in publishing of the 1960s and 1970s, and had not created the infrastructure of writers' organizations, periodicals, literary prizes, public events, and international outreach that supported literary production in French Quebec and in English Canada.

As I went around the city with a tape recorder in 1986 and 1987, I soon discovered that the English writers of Montreal were all but forgotten and thoroughly demoralized. Writers are great grumblers, and there is not always good reason for complaint. The indignation of the time I am writing about was widely shared, though, and well justified. It has also turned out to be productive.

I published some of the writers I had been reading and teaching in a special issue of *Canadian Fiction Magazine* in 1988 that was republished in book form as *Telling Differences: New English Fiction from Quebec*. I published some of the same writers and some different ones in *Matrix* magazine and in the fiction series I edited for Véhicule Press between 1989 and 1995. I was part of a group of writers, publishers, booksellers, and educators who in 1988 created the community organization QSPELL, which gave annual book prizes before morphing into the Quebec Writers' Federation ten years later.

I wrote an essay on *Two Solitudes* in 1990 and published my first novel, *Birds of Passage*, in 1993. I was involved in establishing the first important links between writers' organizations on both

sides of the language divide at Write pour écrire in 1996. And I have been promoting this literature on an international stage at the Blue Metropolis Montreal International Literary Festival since 1999 and in educational programmes that put Montreal writers in touch with students in every region of Quebec and across Canada.

I have been in the thick of it, in other words. As I myself come into the picture — and the "they" becomes a "we" — what I have to say is based on interviews with a few of the writers, as well as my reading, my personal experience, my notebooks, and my memory.

There is some danger in identifying the story of Montreal's literary revival too closely with my own career. The danger is that I will privilege those activities and developments I was involved in and know best.

This can also be advantage. I happen to have been involved in most of the key developments affecting the English Montreal literary scene over the past 30 years. There are some I was not privy to, and it will be up to someone else to write about those. Writing from my own experience has the advantage of revealing the process behind much of what happened.

There are words I have quailed either from defining or from qualifying. *Québécois* is one. Does it refer to Francophones only? Am I myself a *Québécoise*? I am a Quebecer, certainly, and in some contexts Quebecer works as an adequate translation of *Québécoise*. But not all contexts, for being a *Québécoise* is in other contexts charged with an exclusive, nationalist meaning that doesn't apply to people like me who speak English.

So many of the words we use to describe ourselves are problematical. There are writers working in English in Montreal who think of themselves as "English" or "English-speaking" writers, and there are others who object to "English" and prefer "Anglo" or "Anglophone." It being impossible to find any term that will please all the writers I will be talking about, I choose to vary the terms and will be using Anglo, Anglophone, English, and English-speaking interchangeably. Is a Beirut-born novelist an Anglo? I say yes, if he writes in English. What about the Turkish fiction writer who wrote her Ph.D. thesis at McGill in anthropology? Ditto. And is the Hungarian-born essayist who speaks English with her husband and

writes essays and book reviews in English for *The Gazette* an English Montreal writer? In my book, yes, she is one of the English writers of Montreal, and right now she's in my book.

Do English Montreal writers belong to English Canada? To Quebec? Both? Neither? Writing in English from Montreal is part of Canadian literature, yes, but it's from Quebec. It's part of Quebec literature, only it's written in English.

In the early post-war years, Montreal's English-language writers saw themselves as Canadians, but the picture got more complicated with the rise of nationalism. There are writers here who have thought of themselves as belonging to both Canada and Quebec — and who have been dismayed to realize that neither Canada nor Quebec was particularly interested in writing in English from Montreal. The assertion of rival national identities called for clear boundaries, and writers working in English in Montreal were a complication that neither side was in any hurry to claim.[10] We had become writers without a country.

A country can be useful to writers trying to make their way in the world. It can provide practical help in providing writers with readers, for a start, and with respect and recognition, perhaps even visibility and honours. By the time I was going around with a tape recorder in 1986, the English writers of Montreal had none of the above. Some had left Montreal as part of the great exodus of the late 1970s and 1980s. Others stayed on but stopped writing. None chose to write in French, although several include enough French in fictions written in English to make their work seem foreign to readers unused to a mix of languages. There were a few who were not too interested in respect and recognition, and who were happy enough with their lot. Most were demoralized and all but forgotten.

Feeling disadvantaged is an occupational hazard for writers, no matter where they live, and complaints from writers that they are not getting their due mostly fall on deaf ears. What interested me about Montreal writers working in English was not only that I thought some of their work was good, although I knew some of it was good. I also knew good science fiction writers, who had their own grievances, and a few years later I would spend time exploring the fiction of the

Troubles in Northern Ireland, which included other writers I admired. What interested me most about Montreal's English-language writers was that their situation simultaneously provided both more reason for complaint and less reason for complaint than the situation of other writers I knew of. That conundrum, which is what has kept me interested all this time, is at the heart of this book.

English Montreal writers have so much less reason for complaint than most writers on the planet because they write in English in the heyday of global English. In a purely literary context — which is the context in which most writers and literary commentators are comfortable — the situation of English Montreal is not in fact much different from that of any number of other writers or groups of writers working in English. To understand what makes the situation of English Montreal unique we have to step back from the literary world to see the political context within which these writers have been working. That context is the fissure between English Canada and Quebec.

A country can also be an impediment to a writer. Where the advantages to belonging to a national literature are of a practical nature, the disadvantages can be fundamental to the work a writer will produce. When asked about the literary climate in Canada in the late 1970s, Gallant was clear: "I would advise any young writer to keep out of it. Go your own way" (Hancock 1978, 43).[11]

We should have listened to her. Instead, we have complained when passed over for the Governor General's Award or the Giller Prize; when our novel was rejected by McClelland & Stewart or House of Anansi Press; when a French-language publisher decided against publishing a French translation of our book; or when we weren't invited to join a delegation of Canadian or Quebec writers sent to Prague. I know no English Montreal writer who has not at times heartily wished to belong to at least one of our national literatures.

That was not going to be our lot, which is part of the price that those of us who survived the 1980s and 1990s have paid for living in Montreal. For there has been a price. Creative tension, too, of course. No shortage of excitement; if anything, an excess of excitement. Our path, as writers, was going to be tough and lonely, whether we liked it or not, even more tough and lonely than the path of writers elsewhere.

No matter what we wrote, we would have few readers and little in the way of respect, let alone recognition, visibility, and honours.

We English writers of Montreal have been — have had to be — more enterprising, more feisty, and even more dogged than most writers need to be. This is true of our work as individual writers — if indeed we were interested in being published and read — and it's true of the work some of us have done as members of our literary community, as well.

Without necessarily wishing to do so, we have gone our own way. We have had nothing to lose, and that has made us fearless and innovative. Along the way we realized that sitting around waiting for Canada — or Quebec — to shower us with glory was not the way to go. That was just not going to happen, not until — or not unless — we managed to make a mark internationally.

It's the old story: you have to make it in New York or London or Paris in order to get your due at home. That was true in MacLennan's day, and it was understandable in MacLennan's day, for there was no indigenous Canadian publishing industry to speak of in the 1940s.

There is now a vibrant English-language publishing industry centred in Toronto as well as a French-language publishing industry centred in Montreal. So why is it still true of so many writers of English Montreal that they have to make it internationally before they are recognized — or even published — at home?

My story here is the sweep of history as it has affected the fiction written in English by Montreal writers. This will mean touching at times on the poets, whose history overlaps with that of the fiction writers;[12] it will meaning touching at times on writers working in French, whose history is quite different, and on English-Canadian writers from outside of Quebec whose history is different again.

The work of many of these English Montreal fiction writers merits separate essays that are beyond my scope here. In a short survey of a turbulent period of sixty-five years, I will only occasionally pause to analyze a particular text, but much of what I have to say is informed by work others have written on some of them — and on work I myself have done in other contexts on individual writers ranging from Hugh MacLennan and Mavis Gallant to Edward O. Phillips and Gail Scott.

By the early 1980s and into the 1990s, the only English writer living in Quebec who could be sure of a place on the literary map of Canada was Mordecai Richler. He secured himself a place on the literary map of Quebec, too, not for his fiction, but for his scathing comments on Quebec's language laws in *Oh Canada! Oh Quebec! Requiem for a Divided Country*. The rest of us might as well not have existed, for all the impact we were having either in English Canada or in Quebec.[13]

That is when we started the process that has made our mark on the world map. English writers from Montreal have been enjoying a revival in this new millennium, and are today taken as seriously internationally, if not nationally, as they were in the post-war golden age.

Some of us created a uniquely multilingual literary festival to showcase our work. Some of the fiction writers — Yann Martel, Anita Rau Badami, Rawi Hage, Jeffrey Moore, Madeleine Thien, and Miguel Syjuco among them — have won international literary prizes. Some of us — including Ann Charney, David Homel, Irena Friedman Karafilly, Colin McAdam, Heather O'Neill, Edeet Ravel, Claire Holden Rothman, Neil Smith, and Eric Siblin — have found publishers in London and New York, Paris and Belgrade, New Delhi and Shanghai. We may or may not have been aware that we were following in the footsteps of MacLennan and Gallant, Richler and Cohen when we did so, but that is what we were doing.

Individual success in the literary field is the product of many considerations, among which talent and determination rank high, and timing and luck play some part — the receptive agent, or publisher, or critic — as does the language in which a writer works. The change we now see in our collective literary fortune is more, though, than the sum of the individual successes of a dozen or more writers. That kind of change is the product not only of all those individual successes but also of the dramatic improvement some of us writers have made in the practical conditions under which we work.

The process of changing those conditions has been the work of many people. My story includes several stages in that process, from QSPELL and the Quebec Writers' Federation to Blue Metropolis, all of which have played a role in changing our literary fortunes. There has been recognition for English writers and their work in Montreal, with

the Grand Prix du livre de Montréal going to poet David Solway in 2004. There has been recognition for English writers and their work in Quebec, with Mavis Gallant becoming the first writer in the English language to win the Prix Athanase-David in 2006, and with the appearance in 2007 of Michel Biron, François Dumont, and Élisabeth Nardout-Lafarge's revisionist *Histoire de la littérature québécoise*, which allows for the existence of a *littérature anglo-québécoise*. There has been some recognition forthcoming from English Canada, too, with Peter Behrens winning the Governor General's Award for fiction in 2006, the first Anglo to do so since Gallant won a quarter of a century earlier in 1981. After Toronto and Vancouver, English Montreal remains the largest market for English-language books in Canada.

Some of the writers of today believe their successes are entirely owing to their own talents. The other side of that coin is that some of the writers of the 1980s feared that their failure to make their mark was their own fault. We have to ask ourselves if the writers of today are really any more talented than the writers of yesterday.

There are not only talented writers working in English in Montreal today; there are more of us today than ever before. Partly this is because some of us took the time to make this a better place for a writer to be; partly it is because apartments in Montreal are plentiful, rents relatively cheap, and the city appealing. The increased numbers have created a sense of critical mass, but there were talented writers here yesterday, too; many of them are the very same writers. What has changed is not so much the talent of the writers as the context within which they work.

That context has changed not only in practical terms, but also politically. If nationalism shows no signs of abating, it has evolved. English-Canadian nationalism spiked with the Winter Olympics in Vancouver in February 2010,[14] when so many of us were proud of the Canadian athletes, both English-speaking and French-speaking.

Quebec nationalism continues to have the support of some 40 per cent of Francophones,[15] more when there's news of fresh linguistic disasters, such as the lack of French at the Olympic opening ceremonies in Vancouver. Canada and Quebec are no longer striving to assert themselves, however, as they were doing in those dangerous decades between the early 1960s and the 1995 Referendum. Many

battles have been put behind us, even if they were never actually won. Things have settled down in recent years, as Canada and Quebec each demonstrates a more mature confidence in its own identity.

Every time things settle down, of course, someone is sure to lob another blazing salvo into the linguistic tinderbox. Last week it was angry parents protesting the closing of yet another English school. This week it's yet another outraged report in the French press of sales staff addressing customers in English on Ste. Catherine Street. When there's a new scene in the ongoing drama of language legislation, there will be Anglos protesting that the new provisions trample on their rights, and there will be Francophones insisting these changes are a betrayal of the Charter of the French Language. What will come of the latest furor? Probably nothing. There's some kind of furor practically every week, and nothing comes of most of them.

But you never really know when something will. There's always a sliver of anxiety, which is part of the price of living in Montreal. One of the things you learn is that there's no way to know what might start a conflagration. We've all been burned.

Most of these fires die for lack of fuel, for this is not only a complicated city, but a city with an edgy sense of humour. So we roll our eyes and laugh, turning anxiety into a joke. Serge Chapleau draws a cartoon about it for *La Presse*, Aislin for *The Gazette*, and then the two of them appear on stage together to a mixed crowd. There's delight, most of the time, except when they go too far and there's outrage instead.

Whatever has to do with language is the stuff not only of wry amusement but also of political correctness, solemnity, and high seriousness. It has to with the survival of a people, dignity, nation, the future of the French language, the vitality of this French-speaking minority. And of that English-speaking one. You do have to be careful not to talk about both of these in the same sentence. The very idea is sacrilegious.

Hardly surprising, then, that this is the city both of the Just for Laughs Festival and of Juste pour rire, which are not the same thing. How could they be the same thing? One is in English, after all, and the other is in French. Montreal is a great city for other festivals, carnivals, and fireworks, a city in which merriment is taken seriously. The traditional winter carnival has transmogrified into Montréal en

Lumière in February; then it's one festival after another from April to September with Blue Metropolis followed by Vues d'Afrique, Accès Asie, the Franco-Folies, Festival TransAmériques, Montréal Baroque, the Festival International de Jazz de Montréal, the Festival des Films du Monde, and dozens of others. There's even a festival of fireworks.

It's so easy to turn everything that has to do with language into a joke. So easy and so risky, except at carnival time, when everything is permitted, except for what is not permitted, even at carnival time.

3
The Good Old Bad Old Days

When she returned to the city of her childhood at the age of eighteen in 1940, Mavis Gallant worked at a variety of jobs before being hired as a reporter for the Montreal *Standard* newspaper in 1944. "Perhaps because of the work I was doing — I loved being on a newspaper — it was very exciting," she told me in 1987. "I've been dying for someone to write about the 40s."[16]

Maurice Duplessis, who had been premier before the war, returned to power in 1945. The dark years of his repressive regime, which became known as *la Grande noirceur,* would last until his death in 1959. Duplessis was the champion of the right-wing nationalists and defender of the authority of both the Catholic Church and Anglophone-controlled business interests. *Le ciel est bleu, l'enfer est rouge* was his party's slogan: "Heaven is blue, hell is red." Blue was the colour of Duplessis's Union nationale party, red the colour of the Liberal Party of Quebec.

Political opposition was ineffectual since the French and English media were in cahoots with the regime. It was only towards the end of *duplessisme* that the unions started to flex their muscles against a government that had consistently been anti-labour in its tactics and its legislation. William Weintraub graduated with an arts degree from McGill in 1947 and was hired as a reporter for *The Gazette.* "There was villainy abroad in the late 1940s," he told me. "The politics in Quebec were so corrupt, so unjust, for English and French alike,

that there was something to react against. And there's nothing like the feeling of injustice and oppression and corruption to stimulate you."

The excitement came from the whiff of change and an opening up to the world. For Gallant there was no other time like the 1940s:

> It was unique. It was a wonderful, thrilling time to be young. All the old conservative dead weight was still there, and of course French Canada was still locked, but there were elements breaking out, and that was what was so exciting. I'm thinking of the painters particularly, and in a city that size you tend to all know one another — the bohemia. I wonder if I would have said that of any city, but I don't think so, because you couldn't have said it of Toronto in those days And there was something thrilling about Montreal: the two languages, the centre still hadn't been destroyed as it is now, and it was full of shade trees and attractive stone houses and the stone houses had been made into little flats for a lot of artists and writers and young people.

The bohemia was at the centre of the city, in the area that had had its glory days as the Golden Square Mile. Wealthy families that had once lived in the Victorian houses and mansions on these streets between Guy and de Bleury had over a period of decades been moving on. In due course those same houses would — if they escaped demolition in the building boom of the 1960s and 1970s — become gaudily painted annexes of Concordia University or fashionable galleries, boutiques, and restaurants. During the 1940s though, they had been converted into cheap apartments. John Sutherland, founder of *First Statement*, had a room on Stanley Street a little way up from his sister Betty, who married Irving Layton in 1944. Gallant was living on MacKay Street and later moved to Lorne Avenue on the other side of University Street. As she told me:

> People didn't travel during the war, and right after the war you couldn't take $25 out of the country — to stabilize the Canadian dollar — so you couldn't travel. So there was a lot of conversation, endless conversation. Of course that's partly youth. You called on people without phoning. Now I wouldn't even answer the door if I didn't know who was coming. People dropped in, particularly in the downtown part of Montreal where a lot of people knew each other.

On reflection, she added, "If I were in that milieu now, at my age, I wouldn't want to be bothered. I'd want to be writing. But I was at the age where you're 'out'— admiring, *bouche bée*."

In the midst of the bohemia, the mansions and institutions that were the remnants of Anglo privilege were still very much in evidence along Sherbrooke Street. While most of the writers were in open revolt against the Anglo-Scottish Protestant elite, the existence of this dominant class in fact and eventually in the mythology of Quebec society were part of the context out of which they were writing.

This Anglo-Protestant elite had consisted of not more than 2,000 families, who lived in the Golden Square Mile in a manner similar to the British upper classes. Not more than 50 men from these families were truly wealthy, but they were responsible for founding the Bank of Montreal, for building the Canadian Pacific Railway and, profiting from Montreal's natural advantages as a port, creating the major industries of the city and of Canada. They built McGill University, the Montreal Museum of Fine Arts, the Protestant churches, the Royal Victoria and Montreal General Hospitals, the Stock Exchange, and many of the city's other institutions.

They had lost their grip before 1945. Some families lost everything during the Depression, and Toronto pulled ahead of Montreal as the commercial and financial centre of the country. When Hugh MacLennan arrived in Montreal in 1935 there were "For Sale" signs on the mansions of the Square Mile (Cameron 1981, 103). The war itself provided the final blow. A large increase in the graduated income tax had a significant effect, and wartime measures designed to buy labour peace restricted profits. Families that had survived sold their mansions to institutions and moved out.

English remained the language of industry and commerce through the post-war years, and Anglophone Montrealers still controlled key sectors of the national Canadian economy from their Montreal head offices. Jane Jacobs wrote that right up to 1960 the city appeared "to be what it had been for almost two centuries: an English city containing many French-speaking workers and inhabitants" (Jacobs 1980, 11). Anglophones held a disproportionate number of the city's well-paying managerial jobs, and were better paid. "Cozy, back-channel political accommodation between Anglophone

economic elites and Francophone politicians" protected the autonomy of English-language institutions in Montreal and assured that vital English-speaking community interests were respected in Quebec politics" (Levine 1990, 1). The top dogs in Montreal's social structure were "unilingual Anglophones, living in exclusive neighbourhoods and working in corporations catering to English-speaking markets" (25).

Relations between the French and English were often distant, with each typically keeping the other at arm's length.[17] "We had no contact with the French, in the main," Weintraub told me, "little knowledge, not much respect—especially given the different traditions of civil rights and political liberalism." Several of the English-speaking writers were indeed left-wing. Gallant described herself as "an intensely left-wing political romantic" (Hancock 39); F.R. Scott was a founder of the socialist Cooperative Commonwealth Federation (CCF), the predecessor of today's left-wing New Democratic Party; and A.M. Klein unsuccessfully ran for office as a CCF candidate in 1949.

French-speaking Quebec was not only conservative, but it had good reason to resent *les Anglais* and the glaring inequities of the time. Francophones were the ones carrying the "burden" of bilingualism, as well. This meant that it was up to them to speak English in their dealings with the Anglos. English Montrealers typically made little effort to speak French, and some showed open contempt for French speakers, their language, and their culture.

Irving Layton, who had spent a time boarding in a French-Canadian family home when he was a student at Macdonald College in Ste-Anne-de-Bellevue, later wrote angrily about the "revolting arrogance" that other English-speaking students displayed towards the French-Canadians:

> They may have been in Canada no more than 24 hours yet, already, on encountering a French-Canadian student, they would make *him* feel *he* was the foreigner. Reinforcing native obtusement and complacency, their snobbery was a force to be reckoned with. It never became clear to me exactly on what grounds these blazered and crested snobs from Ye Olde Slopshire gave themselves such airs of superiority. Such episodes made me understand the upsurge of nationalist feeling that later took place in Quebec. No doubt of it, they also played an important part in forming my animus against what I saw was

the deadening influence of the English sensibility on Canadian poetry. Everything vital and creative in me revolted against it. My abrasive encounters with these uppity young Englishmen, and the colonized Anglo-Canadians desperately trying to ape them, reinforced my scorn. (Layton 1985, 167)

The wonder, in such a context, is not that the English and French writers were worlds apart in those post-war years. They have always been worlds apart and in most ways remain so to this day, when so much else has changed. The wonder is how much they had in common in those pivotal years after the war. On both sides of town writers and artists felt a sense of creative excitement, and on both sides of town they were in revolt against the status quo.

Bohemian is hardly the word to describe Hugh MacLennan. In comparison with the young Mavis Gallant — skipping around town with poems in her purse — or with an angry young man like Irving Layton, MacLennan was a bourgeois figure, yet he, too, was in revolt against the stuffy old Anglo-Protestant establishment of Montreal.

The son of a Nova Scotian physician, MacLennan was a Rhodes Scholar with a doctorate from Princeton. His career got off to a shaky start during the Great Depression, when he was unable to get a university position and settled for a job teaching classics at Lower Canada College, a private school in Montreal. He was unable, too, to find a publisher for his first two novels, but did then establish himself as a writer in 1941 with *Barometer Rising*, his novel of the Halifax explosion. *Two Solitudes* appeared in New York on the morning of January 17, 1945, and it sold out its first printing of 4,500 copies by noon. MacLennan, aged 33, was on his way to winning the first of what would become five Governor General's Awards — and to becoming the most celebrated Canadian novelist of his day.

His success with *Two Solitudes* was one of several remarkable signs of the vitality of Montreal's literary scene at the time. All the more remarkable, given that there was no indigenous publishing industry interested in the work of Canadian writers. Toronto-born Montreal novelist Gwethalyn Graham won her second Governor General's Award in 1944 for *Earth and High Heaven* (the first had been for *Swiss Sonata* in 1938), and became the first Canadian to become number one on *The New York Times* bestseller list. Joyce Marshall's

Presently Tomorrow was published in Boston in 1946. Marshall herself had moved to Toronto, but her novel was set at a girls' boarding school in the Eastern Townships of Quebec not unlike the one the author herself had attended during the 1930s, and its account of one of the girls' sexuality scandalized several Canadian reviewers, especially "Samuel Marchbanks," the pseudonym of Robertson Davies.

Exposure in the American media and the serious consideration of influential American critics ensured such Montreal writers far greater success than could ever have been hoped for from any Canadian publisher. The 22-year-old Constance Beresford-Howe benefited from American publication when her first novel, *The Unreasoning Heart*, won the Dodd Mead Intercollegiate Literary Prize in 1945; it was published the following year (Leith 1987). These were signs of extraordinary success. In subsequent decades, Canadian nationalists have been critical of the United States for its negative impact on the development of English-Canadian culture. While there is undoubtedly some truth to this, these examples from the 1940s remind us that the effects were not always negative.

The vitality of the period is in fact remarkable. A.M. Klein published *Hath not a Jew...* in 1940 and *The Hitleriad* in 1944; *The Rocking Chair*, for which he won a Governor General's Award, was published by Ryerson Press in Toronto in 1948, and his novel, *The Second Scroll*, by Knopf in New York in 1951. Ralph Gustafson, from the Eastern Townships, was living and writing in New York and publishing his own fiction and poetry as well as influential anthologies of Canadian poetry. Scott, Patrick Anderson, Neufville Shaw, Kit Shaw, and P.K. Page were at the centre of the *Preview* circle in Montreal. Gallant was planning to be a poet — she wrote nothing but poetry until she was 18 or 19 (Hancock 21) — and then started to write short fiction. She was on the fringes of *Preview*, where two short stories of hers appeared in 1944. John Sutherland's little magazine, *First Statement*, was generating interest in the work of Layton and Louis Dudek.

Layton's University Street apartment was a hangout on Friday and Saturday evenings, and "everyone who was anyone" used to come by: Frank Scott, Patrick Anderson, Dorothy Livesay, A.J.M. Smith, Dylan Thomas. There was a café, too, on de Bleury south of Ontario

where Layton knew he would run into Louis Dudek and John Sutherland and Audrey Aikman. And of course he was writing. His first book, *Here and Now*, was run off on the *First Statement* printing press that he bought with his army discharge money in 1945. The city "gave me the confidence, the tools, the stimulating friendships and rivalries. It gave me a literary milieu comparable to what Paris had given the American expatriates, Hemingway and Fitzgerald" (232).

If Montreal had almost everything young writers needed in the post-war years, it was also a great challenge for most of them to find a publisher — and to make ends meet. Layton, and others like Gustafson and Klein, who were writing short fiction as well as poetry in these years, were suffering badly from the lack of response to their work in the United States and, as Layton told me, were "dying of discouragement." Gustafson and Layton eventually abandoned prose fiction altogether, finding it was easier to make an impact with poetry, in part because a little magazine or a chapbook could be produced and distributed at low cost.

Not even the promise of a steady income, however, could lure Layton away from Montreal. When he was offered a teaching job in Winnipeg in 1946, he turned it down. "I felt as if I'd been clubbed by this unforeseen job offer that would take me out of this misery, but also out of Montreal and the stimulation which was now as necessary as the air I breathed" (Layton 251).

Even those with commercial publishers found the financial rewards meagre. MacLennan was happy to quit his teaching job at Lower Canada College after *Two Solitudes* appeared, but there were lean years ahead, thanks to American publishing contracts and Canadian tax law, which did not allow for income averaging. He returned to teaching in 1951, taking up a position at McGill, where he remained until his retirement.

There was excitement on the French side of town, too. It would be years before the new broom of the Quiet Revolution would sweep through Quebec in the 1960s, but a window had opened up in French-Canadian society at the end of the war, and it would never close again.

Quebec fiction had traditionally celebrated and idealized the rural way of life. That changed when journalist Roger Lemelin

appeared on the literary scene in 1944 with *Au pied de la pente douce*, which met with resistance and was refused a literary prize because it was not focused on the countryside (Shek 1977). When, at the same time, Germaine Guèvremont's successful novels *Le Survenant* (1945) and *Marie-Didace* (1947) contrasted the stifling rural way of life with the liberating outside world, it was clear that a new wind had begun to blow through French-Canadian writing. If Lemelin provided the realism, and Guèvremont the poetry, Manitoba-born Gabrielle Roy was the writer who combined both qualities in her first novel *Bonheur d'occasion*, which appeared in 1945 (Coleman 1993, 16).

Some of these Francophone writers had their own impressive international connections. Lemelin was a Canadian correspondent for both *Time* and *Life* between 1944 and 1952. A Guggenheim Foundation fellowship provided him with the time to write his second novel, *Les Plouffe*, which appeared in 1948 and formed the basis for a popular CBC series in French and in English in the early years of Canadian television. The original French version of *Bonheur d'occasion* won Roy the prestigious French *Prix Femina* in 1947, and the English translation, *The Tin Flute*, won the Royal Society of Canada's Lorne Pierce Medal and the 1947 Governor General's Award for fiction; this was for the English translation, since there were no awards given for writing in French until 1959. The novel also sold more than three-quarters of a million copies in the United States when the Literary Guild of America made it a feature book of the month.

The artists and writers associated with painter Paul-Émile Borduas and the iconoclastic 1948 manifesto *Refus global* had been influenced by surrealism, especially in France. Their revolt against a deeply repressed Quebec had no equivalent in English Canada, and it had none of the popular appeal of the new realist novels. In their embrace of life, risk, spontaneity, love, and freedom, though, they constituted a spectacular unofficial opposition, and for them, too, this was a time of extraordinary effervescence. As the multi-talented poet, painter-engraver, and publisher Roland Giguère said in an interview in *La Barre du jour* two decades later, "I believe it was our Golden Age. Without a public, without galleries and publishers, without anything except beautiful, youthful revolt, we had so much to do and we did it all" (Théoret and Stafford 1967).

Gallant was one of the rare individuals who walked between these two worlds, for she spoke French fluently and had an exceptional understanding of French-speaking Montreal. Her unconventional Anglo-Protestant parents had not only put her in the care of a French-Canadian nursemaid when she was a small child, but had packed her off to a French Catholic boarding school. Her job at the *Standard* gave her a lot of freedom, and she was able to convince her editors to run features on "French-Canadian topics" such as Gabrielle Roy's *Bonheur d'occasion* and a day spent trailing around after Premier Maurice Duplessis himself.

The translators — A.M. Klein, F.R. Scott, and John Glassco, whom Layton described as "a presence, though only a ghostly one" (Layton, 248) — were the ones most aware and most appreciative of the poetry that appeared in French. There was sufficient interest in English-Canadian fiction that it was regularly reviewed.

Two Solitudes is the key text in Canadian nationalism of the period, and its reception in French speaks to the very differences that are its subject. It had some enthusiastic reviews and some critical ones, and was undoubtedly read in English by some Francophones, but its publication was far from an event in French Canada. The novel did not appear in French until 1963, and then in an edition published not in Montreal but in Paris. Canadian nationalism — and an English-Canadian's view of the relations between the French and English of Canada — had much less traction in Quebec than elsewhere.

The Canadian publishing world was gradually waking up to the opportunities provided by Canadian fiction as a result of MacLennan's success and that of other Montreal novelists. Such Canadian publishers as were issuing trade books, fiction, poetry, and history were all in Toronto in the 1940s (Whiteman 1994, 65). John Gray, who joined Macmillan as managing editor in 1946 and became president within a year, had been very impressed by *Two Solitudes* when a friend sent him a copy in Europe at the end of the war. He and Jack McClelland of McClelland & Stewart were fired with the energy and enthusiasm required to transform the publishing industry. The Massey Report in 1951 and the establishment of the Canada Council in 1957 provided the support they needed.

MacLennan signed with John Gray in 1949, and Macmillan became increasingly important to him thereafter not only because of his personal friendship with Gray but also because MacLennan terminated his longstanding relationship with Duell, Sloan and Pearce in New York. By the mid-1950s, Canadian writers who would previously have looked to New York to sell their manuscripts were eyeing Toronto with interest.

The connections between the worlds in which writers live and the kind of work they write are complex and unpredictable. There are links, surely, between the decline of the Protestant ascendancy in Ireland and the work of William Butler Yeats, say, or that of Samuel Beckett, but what are those links? Can we imagine William Faulkner emerging out of any other world than that of the American South? And if we cannot, well, what can we say about the impact of that particular context on his fiction? Are there ways of broaching such a topic without reducing and trivializing the individual writer? No matter how well we think we know a writer, we know so little of what lies behind the text. There are good reasons why literary criticism is wary of commenting on the link between a writer and his milieu.

What we can do is remark on what is written and published, and sometimes we can put that alongside what we know of the writer and his world. Here is the text, which has these characteristics, some of which it may share with other texts by the same writer or other writers. And here is what we know about the writer, the time, and the context.

A.M. Klein's *The Second Scroll* (1951) is a novel that would be exceptional in any literary company, with its unique combination of innovation and tradition, of Joyce and Judaica. Brian Moore's *The Lonely Passion of Judith Hearne* appeared in 1955 and *The Feast of Lupercal* in 1957. Richler launched his career with novels written with a jumpy incongruity new to Canadian fiction. *The Acrobats* appeared in 1954, *Son of a Smaller Hero* in 1955, and *A Choice of Enemies* in 1957. Sometimes adventurous in their use of stream-of-consciousness, fragmentation, and other modernist narrative techniques, these writers had the effect of broadening interest in Canadian fiction at home and internationally.

Gallant, who had moved to Europe in 1950 to be a writer, started publishing short fiction in *The New Yorker* in 1951. "Bernadette,"

which tells the story of a well-to-do English-speaking Montreal couple unaware of their French-Canadian servant's pregnancy, is a richly comic story written after a long return visit to Montreal. First published in 1957 and reprinted in *My Heart Is Broken* (1974), the story is merciless in its send-up of Nora Knight's mix of self-interest and self-righteousness. It is also a remarkable fictional anticipation of the changes Quebec would be undergoing after Duplessis died in 1959 and the implications of those changes for English-speaking Montrealers like the Knights.

Nora, whose "weapons were kept sharp for two dragons: crooked politics and the Roman Catholic Church" (15) has always been applauded for her "leadership." In her element at a dinner party which includes some her "ethnic treasures" and three journalists representing "French Canada," Nora makes the mistake of boasting that Bernadette has been reading books by Gide and Colette. When Bernadatte's naïve Catholicism makes a mockery of this claim, the party goes wrong and Nora ends up feeling "outside the party." That is a feeling that was about to become familiar to many English-speaking Montrealers.

At the end of this post-war period, in 1959, Hugh MacLennan published *The Watch That Ends the Night* and Mordecai Richler *The Apprenticeship of Duddy Kravitz*. Over a period of 15 years, the English fiction of Montreal writers had been moving away from the majestic confidence of the opening of *Two Solitudes* to the formal expression of anxiety. While Richler was hitting his edgy stride, there was only so far that MacLennan could be expected to stray from the classical style he lived and breathed. The distance travelled between *Two Solitudes* and *The Watch That Ends the Night* is nonetheless remarkable. Here is the tentative opening sentence of the later novel:

> There are some stories into which the reader should be led gently, and I think this may be one of them.

Instead of the godlike omniscience of *Two Solitudes*, here MacLennan has a modest and uncertain first-person narrator who often says "may" and "might," "suppose" and "seem":

> Now I suppose I should introduce myself. My name is George Stewart and I come from what might be called an old Montreal family.

George is a man who has "never felt safe" and who is riddled with doubt and regret. He infuses the entire narrative with ordinariness and humanity, with the result that *The Watch That Ends the Night* is the best-loved of MacLennan's novels. Another reason for the novel's appeal is that it chronicles the death of George's wife, as indeed MacLennan's own wife Dorothy Duncan was dying at the time. MacLennan himself made the connection between first-person narration and the "times of chaos" he was living through. "In times of chaos," he wrote to John Gray, "we fall back on the only thing we can know for sure — our own responses — and we trust a writer who at least appears to be doing the same. And the present time is surely chaotic" (Cameron, 262).

On the surface, things were as they had always been in the Quebec of 1959. The old regime and its unholy alliance of the state, the clergy, and business interests controlled by powerful English-speaking Montrealers[18] was still in place. But the unions were agitating. A new educated elite was emerging. Change was overdue.

1959 was the year that a young writer from Quebec City named Marie-Claire Blais, then aged 18, published her first novel, *La Belle Bête*, which went on to win the Prix Femina, as *Bonheur d'occasion* had done in 1945. This surreal tale of a pampered and beautiful boy, his bitterly envious sister, and their mother, whose face is being eaten away by cancer, was a perversion of the rural novel and a shocking rejection of what had been.

On September 7, 1959, Maurice Duplessis died. Montreal was about to change dramatically, and with it the literary landscape.

4

Nationalism and Its Discontents

It was June 1963 when I found myself in a big house in Pointe-Claire village west of Montreal with my itinerant family. I had left Northern Ireland when I was a small child in the early 1950s. My father, who was a doctor, had left general practice in Northern Ireland to become editor of *Medical World* in London in the early 1950s, and we had moved to Basel when he was appointed medical director of a multinational pharmaceutical company in 1956. I spoke the local Swiss German dialect with my friends in Basel and Hochdeutsch at school, and I forgot much of both when we moved back to London three years later. I was now 13 years old, and we had come to Montreal because my father had moved to another multinational pharmaceutical company and was now medical director for Canada.

There were many reasons why I felt distanced from this new world I now found myself in. There were things I could not talk to anyone about, for a start.[19] That was part of the distance I felt. I had no history in this place, either. I was a grown woman before I could identify some aspects of Quebec village life with the Northern Irish world in which I had been born. And most of the people living in Pointe-Claire village spoke French.

I don't remember a time when German sounded foreign to me, but I do remember my astonishment, at the age of seven, when I first heard French on a weekend visit to Alsace. In London I had been studying French at school in the two years before we moved to

Montreal, but that was a domesticated, English version of French quite unlike what I remembered from Strasbourg. Quite unlike what I now heard in Pointe-Claire village, too.

Newcomers like me and my family were not the only ones cut off from the French-speaking world; most of the people we knew in Pointe-Claire spoke English and only English. The distance I felt was not only from the French-Canadians whose families had lived in the village for generations and whose language I did not yet understand, but also from my English-speaking classmates. They had been living here for years, but the only place they spoke French was in French class with Mr. Laine. Outside of class, he was addressed as Mister and not as *Monsieur*, and Laine was pronounced as though it were Lane. Though there were several good reasons why I was disconnected from the world I now found myself in, what was really odd was that I was not much more disconnected from this world than everyone else I knew.

Pointe-Claire is the prettiest of the villages on the Lakeshore, with a grey stone church down by the water and a large convent — the Congrégation de Notre-Dame — and a stately old windmill on the point of land that stretches into Lac St-Louis. There were nuns on the streets of the village when we first lived there in 1963 but, within a year or two, they had gone, and it was as though they had never been. This was the Quiet Revolution, and the same change was taking place all over Quebec in those years as the Catholic Church quietly faded from view.

Other changes were less visible but no less profound. The Liberal Party of Quebec under leader Jean Lesage had been elected in 1960 on a platform of change — their campaign slogan was *C'est le temps que ça change* — and instituted a series of sweeping reforms that would create a modern, secular state. The Church had always been responsible for health care and for education. Now, a provincial hospitalization scheme was created along with wholesale educational reforms. Departments of Cultural Affairs and of federal-provincial relations — firsts in Canada — came into being along with the Société générale de financement. Quebec made demands to be recognized as equal in Confederation, demands for the transfer of powers from the federal to the Quebec government, and demands for control over

the economic, social, and administrative means that would allow its aspirations to be realized.

Journalist René Lévesque had moved into politics on the death of Maurice Duplessis, running for the Liberals; he was now Minister of Natural Resources. Lesage called for a new election in 1962 — this time the slogan was *Maîtres chez nous* — to seek a mandate to nationalize Quebec's electric companies. The Liberals were returned to power with an increased majority in the National Assembly, and Lévesque enacted his plans for Hydro-Québec. The Ministry of Education was created in 1964, the Quebec Pension Plan in 1965, and the Caisse de dépôt et de placement in 1965. There were electoral and social reforms, too, including a provincial family allowance scheme implemented in 1967.

My teachers and the parents of some of my school friends may have been happy to see these changes; like many other Quebecers they were unhappy with increased taxes, heavy borrowing, and demands on the federal treasury. The Quiet Revolution had been proving "inordinately expensive" in a province that had been unaccustomed to paying taxes. "Many a farmer and rural tradesman found his tax bill tripled over what it had been in the bad old days of Duplessis" (Fraser 1967, 206). When the Lesage Liberals went back to the polls for a third mandate in 1966, they were defeated.

Montreal was still the urban centre of English Canada in the 1960s. Corporate boardrooms, such as that of my father's office, often functioned in English. This was just as well for my father, whose French never did progress much beyond ordering a good bottle of wine in Alsace.

In spite of the fact that the population of Quebec was predominantly French-speaking, many of the best neighbourhoods were inhabited by English speakers. Downtown Montreal was festooned with billboards and commercial signs in English. New immigrants were more likely to integrate into the English-speaking minority community than into the French-speaking majority (Levine 7).

None of this had been much contested before; it was now contested. Alarm bells were sounding about the future of French. By the 1960s it was clear that French speakers were in danger of

ultimately becoming a demographic minority within Quebec itself. Where 14 or 16 children had been common in French-speaking families, the birth rate was now plummeting. Quebec would have to depend on immigrants for future population growth. With French schools limiting themselves to French-speaking Catholics, however, the great post-war wave of immigrant children was in fact attending English schools (Rudin 1985, 232) and integrating into the English-speaking community.

And what would happen then to the French language of Quebec? Could French flourish in this modern, urban environment with pervasive English influences? Or was French "destined merely to *survive*," as Marc V. Levine put it, "in rural enclaves in a manner akin to the Amish or other 'folkloric' linguistic communities"? That was the burning question. Montreal might always be a bilingual city in terms of its composition, but "nationalists were determined to make French as dominant a language and culture in the city as English was in Toronto or Vancouver" (Levine, 3). And that is what they did in Bill 22, in 1974, which established French as the official language of Quebec, and then with Bill 101 in 1977.

This was a deliberate and conscious turning of the tables: the reconquest of Montreal — to use the unequivocal title of Levine's book — by Francophones resentful of the excessive power and influence of the people who spoke English.

It wasn't only in Quebec that these were momentous years. In Ottawa, Lester Pearson's Liberals were in a tug-of-war with John Diefenbaker's Conservatives in the great flag debate of 1964–65 that replaced the Canadian Red Ensign with the Canadian Maple Leaf. With Quebec nationalism posing a clear threat to national unity, Pearson created the Royal Commission on Bilingualism and Biculturalism to study the widening breach between "the two founding races of Canada." Pierre Elliott Trudeau addressed the Commission at its first hearing in November 1963, stressing the importance of ensuring the equality in law of Canada's two languages to offset the impact that English-Canadian nationalism had had on the development of French-Canadian nationalism:

> I don't mean that in changing laws we will succeed in changing the sociological or political reality — I don't think that's

possible — but I think that the very source of French-Canadian nationalism is a defensive attitude towards an English-Canadian nationalist interpretation of the laws, of the judicial formulas. (Fraser 2006, 87).

What the Commissioners found was so alarming that they prepared an interim report only 18 months after beginning their work. Canada, they wrote, "is passing through the greatest crisis in its history." If it should "persist and gather momentum it could destroy Canada."

The new flag and the Royal Commission were inspired by the belief that the aims and aspirations of French Canada could be satisfied within a changed but still united Canada. For many Quebec Francophones, though, these developments were both too little and too late. By the early 1960s, "separatism" was an openly proclaimed cause (Fraser 201). The nationalists in Quebec were fixing their hopes "not on a reformed Canada, but on a separate or virtually independent Quebec" (Creighton 1970, 337).

Meanwhile, the centenary of Confederation was approaching in 1967 with Canadians troubled over the future of the country. Within Montreal, Mayor Jean Drapeau was building Place Ville-Marie and the Métro system and the Underground City — and welcoming the world at Expo 1967, where many of us sang along to Bobby Gimbey's catchy and bilingual *Ca-na-da* song.

There is something quintessentially Canadian about Expo 67 and its celebration of the city of Montreal, of Quebec, and of the country as a whole at a time of nationalism, for there were very different interpretations of what Expo was all about, and each interpretation was linked with a different political view. "English Canadians may have imagined that Expo 67 was a memorial to Confederation," Creighton comments, but French-Canadians saw it as a demonstration of "the prowess of French Canada" and as "a tribute to the glory of Montreal" (349).

Some Quebec politicians were becoming increasingly radicalized. Lévesque left the Liberals in 1967 when the party refused to debate sovereignty for Quebec. He became the first leader of the Parti Québécois the following year. The flamboyant economist Jacques Parizeau joined Lévesque and the PQ in 1969.

The Quiet Revolution remained remarkably quiet, with the notable exception of FLQ violence. Lesage's duly elected ministers and mandarins were having far more impact in any case than a handful of angry young men. The main struggles took place in boardrooms, party conventions and the National Assembly of Quebec, though there were important skirmishes in the schools, too, where children and their parents bore the brunt of successive laws governing access to education in English.

It was not entirely unanticipated that Quebec's English-speaking population came to feel uncertain of their future in Quebec or that close to 200,000 of them would leave Quebec forever.[20]

I left, too, but not for long, and not for any reason related to Quebec politics. I had moved from high school to McGill, where I studied philosophy. I worked summers at the Manoir Richelieu hotel in Pointe-au-Pic, where I met the Hungarian I would eventually marry. I spent the better part of a year in Brussels (my father had been transferred to Europe) and then Paris, where I studied French language and civilization before enrolling at the University of London for a doctorate on the work of Samuel Beckett. I married my Hungarian, and we returned to Canada together in August 1974.

After one year in Ottawa at Carleton University, my husband was hired by Concordia University and I by John Abbott College in 1975. We loved Montreal and we loved Quebec, and we wanted to make our lives here. The following summer, I was expecting our first child, and we spent two weeks touring some of the areas of Quebec we loved best — île d'Orléans, l'Isle-aux-Coudres, Pointe-au-Pic, Tadoussac — and buying hand-woven *catalognes* for our apartment on Sherbrooke Street. By day we toured seigneurial homes and listened to talks about the history of the original settlers of New France. In the evenings we ate marvelous *cuisine du terroir* and listened to grizzled fiddlers and *chansonniers*.

The hospitable Québécois entrepreneurs we met on our travels must have thought us foreign. My husband's French was accented by Hungarian. They may have been misled, too, by the fact that I spoke French with a slight German or Alsatian accent; odd how one language learned and all but forgotten in childhood can affect the way one speaks another language decades later. I suppose, too, that it

may have been the first time these Quebecers had come across such enthusiastic English-speaking visitors from Montreal, which would not say a lot for the interest other English Montrealers took in rural Quebec.

The local historian on île d'Orléans, who had been talking one afternoon about the impact of the British Conquest of New France, gave us an appraising look and then cooled to us when he figured out that we were English-speaking Montrealers. The Québécois couple we met in the Isle-aux-Coudres hotel the following evening had a similar reaction when they realized we lived in Montreal: an exchange of glances and a turning away. These were minor incidents; they certainly didn't spoil the occasion, let alone the holiday.

Was this nationalism? Was it just an encounter with Quebecers unused to meeting people from "away"? I had no previous experience of nationalism, partly I suppose because nationalism is linked with a sense of belonging, and I had never stayed long enough in one place to know much about belonging. I knew all about not belonging. I had been on the outside all my life. And I was likely more sensitive than usual, having chosen to live here in Quebec, expecting my first baby. All three of my children would be born here. This would be my home. Perhaps it was because I was finally putting down roots that I noticed people taking a step back. Perhaps this is why I still remember these little incidents more than 30 years later.

It was, undoubtedly, a time of nationalism. A few months after that trip along the St. Lawrence, on the evening of November 15, 1976, the Parti Québécois was elected, and René Lévesque became premier of Quebec. I sympathized with the aspirations of Quebec and approved of the Parti Québécois in many ways. I did wonder where all this would lead.

The Charter of the French Language, originally designated Bill 1 — which is a measure of its importance in the nationalist project — and later renamed Bill 101, was enacted in 1977. The law governed such fundamentals as the language of work and public signage, and it restricted access to English schools in various ways. The clause that affected us was the one applying to parents who had had their elementary education outside of Quebec but who were living in Quebec in 1977. If we wished our children to have the right to

English schooling, we would need to be able to prove that at least one of us had had our elementary school education in English. That clause ruled out my child and his brothers, since some of my elementary education had been in German and some of my husband's education had been in Hungarian.

We had always wanted them to go to French school, for fluency in French seemed to us essential, and the French teaching in English schools was inadequate. The way to ensure our sons would learn French properly was to send them to French school, which we did. When some clauses in the law were later softened enough to make our sons eligible for English schooling, I did write letters to my old schools in Basel and London to get the required certificate of eligibility in case our sons or their own children ever wanted to attend an English school in Quebec; two of our sons did in due course have some of their secondary schooling in English.

It is only now, reading Graham Fraser's enlightening book, *Sorry, I Don't Speak French* (2006, 138), that I realize English-speaking Quebecers have never even changed the name of Bill 101 to Law 101, as we should have done when it was duly enacted. That alone says something about our collective alienation from the Charter of the French Language.

I personally had a complicated response, which included not only shock but also a certain equanimity. Philosophically I found Bill 101 hard to accept. As a literary person open to French, open to Hungarian and German and other languages, I found the idea of legislating language shocking. It also felt like an assault on those of us who spoke English, which is surely what it was.

I did understand where the impulse to create such draconian legislation came from, and I understood and accepted the need for change. I did not find the law imposed terrible restrictions on me personally or on my family. I believe it eventually had many positive effects in allowing for the entrenchment of French in Quebec. It may have had some unexpected results, as well. One may be that it has undermined the sovereignist movement by showing that the French language could indeed flourish within the Canadian state. Another may be the creation of the English-speaking Community of Quebec. Anglos who had never before needed to band together — and who

had never before felt themselves to be a minority — did start to band together in the wake of Bill 101.

If I was ambivalent about the law itself, I found something intriguing about its effect. Bill 101 moved English underground. It made English a language we spoke among ourselves, in the privacy of our own homes, and with our intimates and our children.

What mattered most was the language of our children's education, but then we had already decided they would go to French school. We did object to the excessive zeal of some employees of the Office de la langue française, and we had long, interrupted conversations among ourselves and with friends and colleagues in which we looked at the law from all sides, understanding the fear and resentment of English it embodied, laughing at some of the absurdities, getting used to it, dealing with it.

In public, many of us English Montrealers spoke French first and English only later, if at all. Only if the other person had an unmistakably Anglo accent did we break into English. Or if our own French was so halting that the French-speaking Montrealer we were talking to took pity on us and switched to English. We would speak English only with people we knew were also English-speaking, people who would not be offended if we were to say *Hello!* More often, though, we would both continue in French, sometimes not even realizing we were two Anglos speaking French to each other, in the comic opera of language in Montreal.

There were English-speaking Montrealers with experiences that were less friendly and less amusing, either because they could not speak French or because they would not. Many French speakers would react angrily when an English speaker expected them to speak English. Such an expectation on the part of English speakers was a throwback to a time most Francophones were only too glad to have put behind them.

Whatever the language of conversation and exchange, and whatever the emotional charge, English, all-powerful English, was here in Montreal an illicit language. There was something intriguing about that.

Most of my adult life and the lives of my children have been in some way determined by Bill 101. We were living in a society obsessed with language, and an obsession with language had become the new

normal. We were hardly even aware of the extent to which we were becoming obsessed with language. This is the context into which my eldest son grew up. Born in 1976 on the eve of the election of the first PQ government, he was two years old in the year after the Charter of the French Language became law, when he looked at me one day and said, "Mummy, who is Bill 101?"

It was in the late 1970s that I started publishing. It was a good time to be doing this. Thanks to the Canada Council for the Arts, writing and publishing were growing by leaps and bounds both in English and in French. Many of the writers who have become internationally renowned in both languages were just then beginning to make their mark. English-language publishing was now centred in Toronto, with literary presses coming into being in various regional centres, as well, including Véhicule Press in Montreal. French-language publishing was centred in Montreal with a few literary presses in Quebec City and in Francophone communities in New Brunswick and Ontario.

Most of the infrastructure needed to support Canadian literature at home and abroad was put into place during these years: associations of Canadian and Quebec Studies, literary magazines and scholarly publications, the Writers' Union of Canada in Toronto and Union des écrivaines et des écrivains québécois in Montreal, literary prizes including the Governor General's Awards, now open to French- as well as English-language work and, in Quebec, the creation of the Rencontre internationale des écrivains québécois to provide Quebec writers with an opportunity to meet and exchange with writers from elsewhere.

The link between Canadian literature and nationalism is hardly new. McGill professor and publisher Robert Lecker has described Canadian criticism as often being "evangelically nationalist" (2005, 11), and in the late 1960s and 1970s "a pro-national literary consciousness" emanated from House of Anansi Press, which had been founded in Canada's Centennial year (52). One of the most influential books of this time was Margaret Atwood's *Survival: A Thematic Guide to Canadian Literature* (1972). Focused on distinguishing Canadian literature from other English-language literatures — the American,

the British—*Survival* includes just one chapter on writing from Quebec which, in Atwood's reading, appears to have a great deal of similarity to English-Canadian writing except that it happens to have been written in French.

Atwood has also associated herself with a view of Canadian literature that allows room for a Canadian literature in French simply by referring specifically to "Canadian Literature in English" (Atwood and Weaver, eds. 1986). Cumbersome as some of these locutions are, the view of Canadian literature that allows room for French has survived, and not only in academic publishing. There are also many, though, in whose hands writing in French is accorded little place in "Canadian" writing, sometimes no place at all. Hardly surprising, then, that the term Quebec literature, which came into common use during the 1960s, applied only to writing in French.

The Toronto essayist Charles Taylor's *Six Journeys: A Canadian Pattern* (1977)[21] is another text published by Anansi; its view of Canada's "basic Britishness" has the effect of excluding French:

> It is not only that British pioneers and their descendants were largely responsible for the creation of Canada, and are still dominant in our public affairs. It is also that British patterns became ingrained in our culture and have largely determined, for better or worse, the texture of our lives. (iii)

Lecker may be the most avowedly nationalist of contemporary Canadian critics. In the year following the victory of the Parti Québécois in 1976, he declared that he came more and more to understand his commitment to Canadian literature "as a political activity that would assert my own nationalism, my own refusal to accept the separatist agenda as the norm" (52). Working with his Toronto-based partner, Jack David, he set about building the critical journal *Essays on Canadian Writing* and a publishing house, ECW Press, dedicated to Canadian criticism. "I wanted to create a canon as a sign of national value" (94).

The 1970s were a time of soul-searching for English-speaking Quebecers, and many decided they would leave. Toronto especially enjoyed considerable and lasting benefits from the influx of some of Quebec's brightest and best. A total of 197,000 people, most of them

English-speaking, uprooted themselves and left the province between 1971 and 2001 rather than face the tide of Quebec nationalism. This represented some 25 per cent of the pre-1971 population of English-speaking Quebec.[22] The rest of us watched this exodus — we all knew people who left — but chose to stay.

Staying meant adjusting. Staying meant accepting that this was a society in which French was the only official language. Staying meant accepting that English was resented. Staying meant finding a way to make a life for ourselves here that would inevitably be very different from that of the life English-speaking Quebecers had led here before. Very different from the life those who had left would now lead in English Canada. Very different, in fact, from the life of any others, anywhere. It meant facing the unknown.

This was easier for people who were young, educated, and adventurous, and especially for those who were comfortable — or comfortable enough — in French. The faculty of John Abbott College, which had only come into existence in 1970, consisted of men and women of my generation. Not all spoke French; many were prepared to spend their lives in English within the protective shell of an English institution. I was drawn to more adventurous colleagues interested in bringing people from different cultural and political realms into contact with one another.

Bryan Campbell had been educated in English and did not speak French fluently, though his mother and sister were Francophone. He was one of the almost imperceptibly small number of English-speaking Quebecers who believed in sovereignty for Quebec. Bill Tierney, who would later become mayor of Ste-Anne-de-Bellevue, was an English rugby player who had moved to Nova Scotia as a student and had married Bryan's cousin.

They shared an interest in Quebec that appealed to me, and they had the idea of creating a magazine they called *Montreal Review*. When they asked me to be associate editor, I agreed. It was effectively a family business, and I was not part of the family, so this would be a brief association. For the first issue in 1979, though, I wrote a review article on Gallant's Linnet Muir stories set in the Montreal of the 1920s and the 1940s.

In preparing this article, I wrote to Gallant with questions about the stories. I was staggered when I got a reply that suggested

she would sue me if I said anything to suggest that the stories were autobiographical. I sent her a copy of the published article, and she wrote a friendlier reply: "What a relief!" she said, to read my article and find it was not claiming that the character Linnet Muir was Gallant herself. I applied for and received a Canada Council grant to write about her work, and used part of the grant money to travel to Paris to meet her for the first time.

I corresponded with Gallant after that. I spent weeks at the microfiche machine in the antiquated Montreal public library on Sherbrooke Street opposite Parc Lafontaine reading articles from the *Standard*, the Montreal newspaper that Gallant had worked for in the 1940s. I collected copies of uncollected stories from *The New Yorker* and other magazines. In 1981, I planned a visit to the University of Toronto to see the papers she had donated to the Thomas Fisher Rare Book Library.

This was my first visit to Toronto, which was a city that had taken hold of my imagination in the years that I had been immersing myself in Canadian writing. This was where the most accomplished English-Canadian writers of the day were living — writers like Michael Ondaatje, Dennis Lee, Gwendolyn MacEwan, Marian Engel, Margaret Atwood. This was where some of them had boldly published and distributed their own work. This was where they had banded together to start up publishing houses like House of Anansi Press and Coach House Books.

As I write these words on a late summer morning, I have just seen a news story about Atwood's imaginative plans to publicize her new novel, which she will be launching at the Edinburgh International Book Festival. What strikes me about this is how extraordinary Margaret Atwood is. From the very beginning of her career half a century ago until today — and going strong — she has shown the rest of us how to do it.

She has shown us how to write. Atwood has written some of the boldest and most original poetry, essays, and fiction of any contemporary writer. And she has the royal jelly. You can complain about her all you like — and the number of people who do so in private is exceeded only by those who are afraid to do so in public — but you have to hand it to her.

She has shown us how to get published, and the message here is "Do What It Takes." In the early days, that meant publishing herself and then working with others to set up a publishing company that would publish several of them. Once she'd won a few awards and had some success, which did not take long, she moved up the rung to McClelland & Stewart, "The Canadian Publisher," and today, with her choice of international publishers, she continues to be published in Canada by M&S — and to support the Canadian publishing industry.

She has shown us what sorts of things you can write about. You can write a bestseller about themes in Canadian literature; *Survival* sold 30,000 copies in its first year. You can write about the Canadian wilderness. You can write about Canada — backwoods Canada, urban Toronto, small-town Ontario — and people across the planet will be interested.

She has shown us many of the forms in which you can write. And that includes once-despised genres like romance, the comic strip, and science fiction. She is reluctant to use the term science fiction, preferring "speculative fiction," but dystopian novels such as *The Handmaid's Tale*, *Oryx & Crake*, and *The Year of the Flood* are works of science fiction for all that, in the same way as are *Brave New World* and *1984*.

She has shown us how to use new technologies to get yourself and your work noticed. You create a Long Pen in order to make remote book-signings possible. You promote your new novel on Twitter. Creating a performance as a way of promoting a novel — as she has now done, generating plenty of media attention in the process — is hardly high-tech, but blogging about it is. She has shown us how to make the most of being a little old lady who just happens to be a technologically savvy literary superstar.

There would be a Canadian literature without Margaret Atwood, but it's hard to know what kind of Canadian literature it would be. She is the colossus of CanLit, doing everything, reinventing herself often, and drawing positive international attention to herself, her work, and Canada.

And of course — *of course* — she has been the target of resentment and jealousy. We Canadians spend a lot of our time looking over our shoulders and comparing ourselves to others. That does double for Canadian writers, for writers are an envious lot. Atwood

herself recalled in 2003 having to deal with a lot of hostile interviews and reviews from men who "felt threatened by the implicit feminism of the early books," and there has been "jealousy of the prominence she had achieved in Canadian literature" (Potts, 2003).

There's a "Jealous-of-Margaret-Atwood Club" online,[23] and some spectacularly hostile commentary even today, when it would seem that Atwood might be almost beyond resentment, too far removed for comparison with most ordinary literary mortals. Montreal poet David Solway writes critically of Atwood as "the goddess of dullness," "who sums up all that is most depressing and parochial and unadventurous in Canadian life and letters" (Solway, 2009):

> Despite her dowager status in Canlit, Atwood is a writer who, with very little in the way of linguistic flair and visionary intensity, writes (or wrote) a kind of period poetry that gives the impression of having long passed its "best before" date. As with most of the characters in her novels, so with the words in her poems: predictable, unvarying, wooden, truncated, connotatively flaccid, oddly nasal in their timbre, and devoid of real signifying power because relying for their effect on a near-perfect correlation with the cultural temper of an audience desperate for corroboration.

Atwood has not always lived in Toronto, but she has chosen to identify herself with the city, and has been a champion of Toronto in public pronouncements as well as in her support for key Toronto-based institutions like the International Festival of Authors, the Writers' Union of Canada, PEN Canada, and the Writers' Trust. She is a writer with a keen appreciation of the advantages of a country — and of the literary capital of that country.

By the time of my first visit to Toronto in 1981, I had read a great deal about how Toronto writers had created a world in which they could flourish. There was something enormously appealing to me about the grassroots literary activism that had turned Toronto into the literary capital of English Canada. I reserved my train ticket with a sense of pleasure and anticipation. I checked into a budget hotel on Yonge Street. I read a review of a restaurant where the food was the palest pink and cream and green. I booked myself a table.

And Toronto was certainly impressive. The big magazines like *Saturday Night* and book industry publications *Books in Canada* and *Quill & Quire* were based in Toronto, as were the large-circulation newspapers *The Globe and Mail* and *The Toronto Star*. That was where influential alternative magazines like *Canadian Forum* and *This Magazine*, and "little" literary magazines like *Tamarack Review* and *Canadian Fiction Magazine* had emerged as important voices for the Canadian nationalism of the day. When it came to English-Canadian writing, Toronto was where it was at.

I sat in the flawlessly modern Thomas Fisher Rare Book Library, where the only sound was the whirr of a pencil sharpener, and compared this to shabby old McGill and its dog-eared catalogue cards. I met Gallant's publisher Douglas Gibson, who spent a companionable hour with me in his office at Macmillan. I met Geoff Hancock, editor of *Canadian Fiction Magazine*, who had published a long interview with Gallant that remains, to this day, one of the most informative and interesting ever to appear.

Hancock and I had a certain amount in common, as literary people of the same generation sharing an interest in Mavis Gallant at a time when there were not many Canadians who knew her work. Our conversation was pleasant enough, but it was not a conversation among equals. I was conscious of his considerable influence — his magazine was then at its peak — and of my own inexperience. He clearly had had doubts about meeting me, for he had set out a row of large pebbles on the coffee table between us. At the end of our conversation, I asked him about the pebbles. "If you had turned out to be a boring person," he told me, "we would have talked about them."

We all have a Toronto in our lives. For the three sisters in Chekhov's play, it was Moscow. Moscow was what they aspired to, what they longed for. Those of us who are writers may long to be part of New York or London or Paris. We want to be the toast of the town. Canadian writers from all over the country dream of Toronto.

For many writers living elsewhere, "Toronto" is an idea: the idea of success. Many Canadian writers are under the impression they would be more successful than they are if only they lived in Toronto. Some of this is wishful thinking, but there are also some good reasons for Canadian writers in other parts of Canada to think this. It does

give a writer a boost to be able to attend those book launches and parties, to get chummy with the publishers and agents and literary journalists, to see and be seen by the people who make the decisions about what gets published, what gets reviewed, who gets interviewed, and who will win the coveted prizes.

"Toronto" — as viewed from elsewhere in Canada — is partly a real city made up of actual institutions and individuals, and partly a city that bears the burden of many Canadians' hopes, desires, and disappointments. If Toronto is the idea of success to many Canadian writers, Toronto has an uncertain place in the hearts of Canadians, literary and otherwise. One of our favourite sports is Toronto-bashing. Toronto is too big and too flat and it tries too hard. It's much like just another American mid-western city, except that it thinks of itself as "world class."

Montrealers never describe Montreal as "world class." Montrealers are generally sceptical about Toronto. Success isn't everything, we say defensively. Montreal doesn't take itself too seriously; it just gets on with the business of living life to the fullest. Most of us Montrealers are happy to be here, and there are lots of other Canadians who wish they could be here, too. I myself come from elsewhere, like many English writers of Quebec past and present, like many other Canadian writers. Even Torontonians wish they could live here, and there are some who have actually moved — or moved back — here.

Few of them are literary types. Given a choice, it's rare for a writer to pass up the advantages of living in Toronto. The only two former Montrealers I know who moved here did so because life in Montreal for an English-language writer is so quiet and uneventful that they're able to write in peace. This is the reason writers who live in London move to rural France for the summer only. They don't spend their lives there. They flock back to London in September to be within reach.

Migration works mostly the other way, away from Montreal. There always writers living in Montreal and working in English, and there must be some who left for Toronto. So why am I finding it difficult to think who they might be? Zoe Whittall is one. There must be others, but most of the writers I know left Montreal for places with advantages very different from those of Toronto: Ottawa,

Peterborough, Saskatoon, Salt Spring Island, Nova Scotia, the coast of Newfoundland, Provence, London, Abu Dhabi. Toronto seems in fact to be no particular draw. If the idea of Toronto has such power over those of us who live elsewhere, why have more of us not moved there?

Sure, there are advantages to being in Toronto. And yes, it might possibly give a boost to an aspiring writer's career. This is hardly guaranteed, however. Being a writer is tough, no matter where you live, as Toronto writers have good reason to know. And even if there is some advantage to living in Toronto, it isn't enough to persuade most writers to pick up sticks and move.

"Montreal" is an idea, too, for those who live outside of the city. To many Canadians, "Montreal" is the idea of pleasure. There are English-speaking Quebecers living in small regional communities who see the city as a mythic monolith and resent Montreal and its size and power in something like the way that writers living outside of Toronto resent "Toronto."

For those of us who live here, however, Montreal is a real place, and, love it as we may, we see its complexity and its failings. Many of us have lived through years dominated by political battles and periodic flare-ups of intolerance, none of them long-lasting, but disturbing for all that. Most of us Anglos who are still here have taken most of what has happened in stride. We have friends and family here. We feel part of this complicated place. We'd miss it if we were to move. We have a stake in what happens here. The big challenge has always been to make Montreal work for us professionally.

I visited Toronto several times in the mid-1980s and have returned many times since, but never for more than a few days, so I cannot pretend to know the city well. In all my visits, I did not learn much that was useful about what had happened to the writers of English Montreal. That was a history I was going to have to piece together for myself.

Leonard Cohen had emerged as a poet in the late 1950s when he was still a student at McGill, and he published two experimental novels, *The Favourite Game* (1963) and *Beautiful Losers* (1966) before leaving Montreal to pursue his international career as a singer-songwriter. Scott Symons had an impact with another experimental

novel, *Place d'Armes* (1967), which is set in Montreal although Symons was a Toronto writer who lived here only briefly.

MacLennan was still living in Montreal, of course, and the reception of his 1967 novel *Return of the Sphinx* is an indicator of the decline of English writing from Montreal in English Canada, for Canadian critics not only trashed the novel, but did so with such hostility and disrespect as to suggest a fundamental rethink of MacLennan's place in Canadian literary history.

Writing in the *Toronto Star*, Robert Fulford described the novel as "the saddest novel of our Centennial summer," while the young Peter Gzowski in *Maclean's* went so far as to cast doubt on MacLennan's ability to write; he compared the novel to Jacqueline Susann's *Valley of the Dolls* (quoted in Cameron 1981, 332-3). It was "kicking season," as MacLennan himself would describe this time. "The few Canadian reviews that did praise and recommend the novel...fell by the wayside in the combination of virulent attack and melancholy disappointment" (Cameron 335). MacLennan had predicted this, blaming it on the "truth" in the novel that Canadians were not ready to face.

The book's reception in the United States was positive. Sales were good (11,000 in Canada, 16,000 in the United States in the first three months alone), but less than half of what had been expected. The final blow was that the Governor General's Awards decided there would be no award for fiction in English that year (340).

In her biography of MacLennan, Elspeth Cameron argues that the timing of the novel's publication was responsible for some of the bad press in Canada. "The fact that it simply happened to coincide with Expo 67 did not help. Many reviewers assumed that he had deliberately produced his book as a kind of contribution to the general flag-waving activities of the Centennial year" (337). MacLennan had indeed associated himself with the festivities by writing the text for *The Colours of Canada* as well as for the new Place des Arts brochure and CBC Radio broadcasts about the Centennial (337). Nationalism, which had helped MacLennan's career as a writer 20 years earlier, came close to ending it in 1967. The effects of the novel's reception in Canada, he confided to John Gray, "could last the rest of my life and come close to driving me out of writing in Canada. No kidding, it could" (340).

It was cold comfort to MacLennan that neither of the other two significant novels of the day — Leonard Cohen's *Beautiful Losers* and Scott Symons's *Place d'Armes* — won or was even shortlisted for a Governor General's Award either. By the late 1960s, when it was kicking season for MacLennan, English writing in Montreal was unable to live up to the spectacular successes in its own past. Some of the novels of the time — Ann Charney's autobiographical novel *Dobryd* (1973), Trevor Ferguson's experimental *High Water Chants* (1977), and work by the prolific Hugh Hood, who published *The Swing in the Garden*, the first in his New Age series, in 1975 — were well received critically but had far less impact than the work of their predecessors.

Writing in English from Montreal was being overshadowed by the upsurge of literary activity in Toronto and other parts of English Canada, on the one hand and, on the other, by the fervour that gripped Montreal writing in French in the wake of Michel Tremblay's *Les Belles-Soeurs* (written in 1965 and staged in 1968), Hubert Aquin's *Prochain épisode* (1965) and Jacques Godbout's *Salut Galarneau!*, which won the Governor General's Award for French-language fiction in 1967.

The poets were the first writers of English Montreal to realize that something had to be done. As in the past, poetry was relatively cheap to publish and distribute, and there were English-language publishing houses for poetry in Montreal. In the 1970s the group known as the Vehicule poets — Ken Norris, André (later Endre) Farkas, Stephen Morrissey, Tom Konyves, and Claudia Lapp — created a buzz around the Véhicule gallery and set up a national network, inviting poets from other parts of Canada and getting invited to their cities in return. They stayed in one another's houses, ate at one another's tables, and got rides to and from airports and events in one another's cars. Publicity was local and mostly word-of-mouth, often within a single institution like John Abbott College, which is where Farkas and I were colleagues for many years. That was where I first saw Irving Layton, Joe Rosenblatt, Marya Fiamengo, and others.

The fiction writers soon realized they were missing out, and the five who banded together in 1970 as the Montreal Story Tellers Fiction Performance Group — Hugh Hood, Clark Blaise, John

Metcalf, Ray Smith, and Ray Fraser — found an innovative way of finding their own audiences through reading engagements in English Catholic schools across the Montreal area. Blaise, who was married to novelist Bharati Mukherjee, set up the creative writing programme at Concordia University and was one of the most promising of Canadian writers of the 1970s; his fiction from this time was published by Penguin Books Canada and HarperCollins Canada.

In 1976, when he and Mukherjee were planning a stay in India, Blaise hired the distinguished American writer Elizabeth Spencer, who had moved to Montreal with her husband in 1958 and published in *The New Yorker*. She wrote much of her novella *The Light in the Piazza* in the Atwater Library and spent 28 years here before moving to Chapel Hill in 1986. "I wrote much of my best work in Montreal," she told me in 2010, including realist stories ("Jean-Pierre," "I, Maureen") with characters alienated from the world in which they live; some of these show awareness of Montreal's social divisions. Mukherjee, who was a member of the McGill English department from 1966 to 1980, published her first novel, *The Tiger's Daughter*, in New York in 1975 and followed that with *Wife* in 1978.

There were, in other words, writers of stature in Montreal, and a few of them were from elsewhere and were publishing outside of Canada. Unlike many other Montreal writers, they were not dependent on Canadian publishers and reviews.

There have always been writers from elsewhere as well as native Montrealers among Montreal's English writers, and it has always been the case that some of them would in due course move on. MacLennan himself was from Nova Scotia, after all, and Montreal-born writers Gallant and Cohen left to pursue their careers; Moore was from Belfast and moved on to California after his time in Montreal.

Blaise was unusually sympathetic to the changing social landscape. His American father was from French-Canadian stock and his mother's family was English-Canadian, so he saw himself as "the heir to the Two Solitudes." On the linguistic question, he took the side of the Quebec nationalists: so far as he was concerned, "the Frencher the better." He thought it was Canada's duty "to exploit its twin heritage of English and French, its twin tensions of America and Britain" (Struthers 1985, 66-67). His interest in Montreal waned

after he and Mukherjee left the city in 1980, and by the time I spoke to him in 1987, he thought the city a good setting in which to explore cultural division (Leith 1987).

Montreal was problematical for many writers working in English in this period of decline, no matter how sympathetic they were to Quebec's aspirations. Hungarian-born Farkas speaks for many writers of the time:

> I have an immigrant background, and English is not my mother tongue. I don't have any guilt complexes about being part of an elite ruling class. I do, however, share a sense of isolation and alienation with other poets writing in English in Quebec. (131)

In the late 1960s and early 1970s, he said, "we witnessed the metamorphosis of the French-Canadians into Québécois," and the shift of economic and literary focus to Toronto.

> I say we "witnessed" because most English writers in Quebec felt themselves to be outside of what was happening. They didn't feel that they belonged to the English establishment, they sympathized with the *Québécois* but could not deny their own linguistic or cultural roots. Most did not want to, or could not, write about what was happening. (131)

English Montreal had not entirely missed out on the publishing boom of the 1960s and 1970s; the most important of the literary presses that came into being in these years was Véhicule Press, which focused on poetry and non-fiction and published fiction rarely. No one was publishing fiction in English on a consistent basis, which meant that the fiction writers looked elsewhere to find a publisher. Most of the fiction writers looked to Toronto, and Toronto was more interested in Francophones. "They were the ones the rest of Canada was curious about," Farkas said. "That is all well and good, but when the corollary is that no notice is taken of the English writing community, then you become frustrated" (Norris 132). One of the Montreal Story Tellers, John Metcalf, complained that their books were not available in Montreal book shops, the universities showed no interest in inviting them to read, and that the doyen of local literary journalists, John Richmond, refused to acknowledge their existence (Struthers 24).

Montreal had become a discouraging place to be writing in English, and for a few years in the late 1970s, very little fiction in English was published by Montreal writers. It resurfaced in 1979 with William Weintraub's *The Underdogs*, which cast a Swiftian look on the future of Anglophones in an independent Quebec, and with MacLennan's own venture into dystopian fiction in his last novel *Voices in Time* (1980), which looks back on the October crisis of 1970 and Hitler's Germany from the post-apocalyptic vantage of Montreal in 2039.

I had already been interested in English Montreal writers. I admired the work of the great Welsh critic Raymond Williams, too, and especially his masterpiece *Culture and Society*. I had developed an interest in science fiction ten years before while taking the first course in the subject ever offered at a Canadian university, taught by Darko Suvin at McGill. I was a consultant on the scholarly journal *Science-Fiction Studies* and had taught a course on Utopian and Anti-Utopian Fiction.

The appearance of these works of dystopian fiction in Montreal in the wake of the social upheavals we had all lived through brought all these interests together. I came up with a research project on English Montreal fiction and proposed it to the Quebec research funding agency. My proposal was deemed "vast," and my application was successful. I set up a home office, cleared space for bookshelves, and bought a tape recorder. I had three years to focus on English Montreal fiction, and I knew I had my work cut out for me.

5

A Case Study in Marginality

René Lévesque had made a commitment to Quebecers to hold a referendum on sovereignty-association, and in 1979, his government made public its constitutional proposal in a white paper entitled *Québec-Canada: A New Deal. The Québec Government Proposal for a New Partnership Between Equals: Sovereignty-Association.* The referendum took place on Tuesday, May 20, 1980, and the federalist side, led by Prime Minister Trudeau, won 59.56 per cent of the votes.

This did not settle the question, for Trudeau had promised Quebecers constitutional change, and the Parti Québécois was returned to power in 1981. The English-speaking community had not waited for the results. They had seen the writing on the wall, and it was in French. Economic opportunities even for bilingual and highly educated Anglophones were scarce in the Quebec civil service. Head offices that employed Anglophones moved west, mostly to the Toronto area. Many families left Quebec, and many young people left on their own, to the enormous and lasting benefit of Toronto.

It was by this time clear that the future of Canada was inextricably linked to the linguistic upheavals of Montreal.[24] The extent to which Francophones felt culturally secure and "in control" in Montreal would go far in determining whether they felt at home in Canada. "Those were perhaps the ultimate stakes in *la question linguistique*" (Levine 6). The one area in which Francophones would not budge was Bill 101. *Touche-pas à la loi 101 !*

What remained of the English-speaking community lurched between despair and defiance as it slowly came to terms with the fact that it was a minority within Quebec. Alliance Quebec, which was created in 1982 as a lobby group, was the most prominent of the organizations created to defend the interests of this minority. If the continued existence of Canada as a single state depended on linguistic peace in Montreal, however, Alliance Quebec was in for a rough ride. Politically federalist and dependent on funding from the federal government, Alliance Quebec was of course in favour of national unity. That interest was consistent with the interests of Anglophones to a point, but only to a point.

With language the hot-button issue for Francophones, national unity depended to a large extent on letting the Francophones have their way on language issues. The interests of national unity diverge from the interests of English-speaking Quebecers in some important ways, however, especially with regard to language. This is a dilemma that long predates Alliance Quebec. Frank Scott had realized in his work on the Royal Commission on Bilingualism and Biculturalism in the mid-1960s that there was a real danger of selling out the English-speaking community of Quebec in order to please Francophones (Fraser 2006, 52). National unity will always trump the interests of English Quebec. Little wonder, then, that English-speaking Quebec has developed a sense of isolation and alienation not only from Quebec, but also, in some measure, from the federal government of Canada and from its own leadership.

Alliance Quebec ran into criticism from angry Anglophones for its supposed unwillingness to challenge the Quebec government. Frustrated English-speaking critics dismissed it as "the lamb lobby" and as "Compliance Quebec" (Richler 1992, 38). On the other side of the language divide, though, Alliance Quebec had a very different image. Even in those early days, the legal challenges that Alliance Quebec was launching against Bill 101 were branding it as an extremist organization among Francophone Quebecers.

It was an extraordinary time. There was a great deal of disruption, not to mention bewilderment and angst. But time passed, and we went on to live through other extraordinary times. We were lucky, in many ways. There was very little violence. In comparison

with other revolutions, this one was quiet. From the point of view of many English-speaking Montrealers, it was clearly a decline. From the point of view of most French speakers, it was a necessary and long overdue correction.

By the mid-1980s, Montreal had been "reconquered" by the French-speaking majority, to use Levine's warlike language (2). In the wake of three language laws and two decades of agitation over the places of French and English in the city, Montreal had undergone what Levine describes as a "stunning transformation." Apostrophes were removed, and Eaton's became Eaton and Nick's became "Chez Nick." A European delicatessen in Pointe-Claire was reported to the Office québécois de la langue française for having greetings on its window in more than a dozen different languages. The Montreal that Jane Jacobs had seen as the "English city" had changed into a city in which French was predominant. Surrounded by French, we got used to seeing French, and so unused to seeing English that it was now disconcerting to visit cities in which English was displayed in public. Toronto seemed like a foreign city.

The English writers of Quebec were reeling. Peter van Toorn described the situation as one of "cultural dereliction" (1982, 34); others spoke of alienation and frustration. T.F. Rigelhof was "sad, lonely, melancholic, chronically depressed" in 1983 after the publication of his first novel, *The Education of J.J. Pass*: "Does anyone die," he asked, "because a first novel that has been enthusiastically reviewed isn't a runaway success with the reading public?" (Rigelhof 2000, 130). Rigelhof does not connect his "*tristesse*" with the fact that he was writing in English in Quebec.

It is one of the great ironies of the time that two English Montreal writers actually won Governor General's Awards in 1981: Mavis Gallant for her collection *Home Truths: Selected Canadian Stories* and Frank Scott for *The Collected Poems of F.R. Scott*. Hugh MacLennan's *Voices in Time* had been passed over, but Elspeth Cameron's biography *Hugh MacLennan: A Writer's Life* was shortlisted for the non-fiction award that same year. Scott had also won in the non-fiction category in 1977 for his *Essays on the Constitution*. It is ironic that neither Gallant (aged 60) nor Scott (78 years old in 1977 and 82 in 1981) had won or was even shortlisted for any such Canadian award at any

other point in their careers. The timing of these honours to writers identified with the Golden Age served not to bolster English writing in Montreal at its nadir but rather to underline the decline from the glorious past to the inglorious present.

Concordia University was one of the few hubs of literary activity in Montreal in these years, and it is thanks to members of the English department there that we have a record of fiction that might otherwise not have survived.

The *Journal of Canadian Fiction* was housed in the Department, and editor John Robert Sorfleet reveals some of the excesses of the time when he overstates both the numerical strength of English Quebec (he includes all non-Francophone Quebecers) and its importance in Quebec literature in a special issue devoted to "The English Fact." Without its English-languages writers, he argues, "the reading of Quebec literature is like sitting down to a meal without realizing that half the meat and most of the seasoning is missing" (Sorfleet 1980, 5).

In a collection featuring several unknown writers, the most significant of the contributors are Henry Beissel and Gail Scott, but both are unsteady at best in their handling of topical and sensitive contemporary material. In Beissel's "Patriotic Chatter," an angry and desperate Roger Wyte explains why he must embark on a career as a sniper in Montreal. He rants against bilingualism, saying that "Bilingual education leads to mental retardation and to identity problems that stalk you all your life." He rants against the French language, which is "elegant, narcissistic and effete." He approves of English, which is "simple, earthy and malleable. That's why English is a world language and French'll never be." Wyte is, in short, a caricature of the angry Anglophone who hates French, incendiary material that requires a very sure touch. Unfortunately, "Patriotic Chatter" succeeds mostly in providing a good example of how not to write political fiction.

Politically, Beissel and Scott are poles apart, but their handling of anger and hatred in this collection is similarly unsatisfactory. "Elizabeth Rides Again" focuses on a bilingual, adulterous, and hateful counter-culture ménage of an English-speaking couple with a baby sharing a house in a Francophone Maritime island community with a Francophone couple. When the main English-speaking character,

Elizabeth, hears her husband Peter playing music, "She listened, hating him for it. Hate is strange. She closed her eyes. The music always took her back to the same place. À l'île" (94). She is attracted to the other man, Giroux, a musician and drug dealer who is rolling joints at the kitchen table when a breeze blows the marijuana across the kitchen table. "*Ferme la porte, hostie*," he screams at Elizabeth. "'*Maudite*,' he added to himself. '*Les maudits….*'" Eloquent though the unspoken word "*anglais*" is, Giroux's hostility is clear.

It does not, however, deter Elizabeth from seducing him. Scott does a good job of describing Elizabeth's sexual arousal, but not so good a job of accounting for her interest in a hostile man. Is this self-hatred on Elizabeth's part? It seems so. Is it linked with the hostility Elizabeth herself feels for English oppressors? This is an island "peopled by fleeing French-speaking Maritimers who had nothing left but their language and by shipwrecked fugitives from the Irish potato famine that washed ashore with almost less than that" (90).

It is never clear what Scott thinks of Elizabeth, whose point of view she uses uncritically throughout. When her tryst in the hayloft with Giroux is interrupted by the wails of her baby, Elizabeth dresses quickly and goes to the rescue, feeling "a familiar anger growing inside her for Peter," whom she blames for leaving the child unattended. "He couldn't be trusted with the baby at all" (94). In the hands of a different writer, such anger could be comical under the adulterous circumstances.

This is not a comic story, though, for a local boy dies after getting high, and Giroux has to leave the island to escape a lynching by infuriated islanders. In the end, Elizabeth finds Peter in the living room dallying with a young woman tourist, and when the woman leaves, Peter and Elizabeth go upstairs, "bathed in an aura of helpless rage." The "furies buzzing around her head," Elizabeth imagines beating Peter over the head with an umbrella (104). This, too, has comic potential, but the potential is unfulfilled, mostly because Scott has been too sympathetic to Elizabeth for us to be sure she has turned on her.

Sorfleet's "The English Fact" collection raises some interesting questions about the ways in which writers respond to change. Were the changes that Montreal had seen too recent, in 1980? Was it too

soon to expect writers to have internalized such massive social and political change and turn it into accomplished fiction? Perhaps the writers needed greater distance from the realities of the period. The failings of these stories by two capable writers may indeed have served as a caution to other Montreal writers, who studiously avoided politics in their own fiction of this period.

Poet Gary Geddes, who taught in the creative writing programme at Concordia, set up two publishing houses — the subscription publisher Quadrant in 1980 and then Cormorant Books in 1984 — with his wife Jan Geddes. His interest in the changes taking place in Montreal and his access to writers teaching in the programme — and theirs to emerging writers — resulted in the publication of a series of anthologies of short fiction by Montreal writers that largely avoid the social and political issues facing English-speaking Montrealers in the decade after Bill 101 passed into law.

Saturday Night at the Forum includes not only Robert Allen and Anne McLean (who later published as Ann Diamond), but two other writers better known today under different names: Edeet Ross, who would become an international literary star as Edeet Ravel with her Tel Aviv trilogy in 2003–2006, and Fran Ponomarenko, who uses the pen name Ludmilla Bereshko.[25]

In his brief introduction, *Saturday Night at the Forum* editor Steve Luxton finds "partisan politics is conspicuous by its absence" in the collection (1981, 7). The other collections from these years are *Matinées Daily* (1981), edited by Terence Byrnes, and P. Scott Lawrence's *Souvenirs: New English Fiction from Quebec* (1987), which includes stories by Julie Houghton Keith, Stephen Henighan, Miriam Packer, Ann Diamond, and Roma Gelblum Bross. Avoiding the issues of the day may seem prudent, especially in the light of the Beissel and Scott stories in Sorfleet's collection, but fiction can focus on the here and now without expressing anger and intolerance, as Elizabeth Spencer has shown in some of the stories she has written about Montreal. It is possible, too, that as an American, Spencer felt less personally affected by the Quiet Revolution and was therefore better able to turn it into fiction.

Another collection of the same period, *Stories of Quebec*, includes the work of many of the prominent post-war writers

of Montreal. In their thoughtful introduction, editors Douglas Daymond and Leslie Monkman also remark on the omission from almost all these stories of explicit comment on the changes that had swept over Quebec, but they notice, too, "a tone of foreboding and fear for the future." Pervasive images of human isolation are reinforced by "the separation of Anglophone communities from the Francophone culture of Quebec" (1980, 7). Dead and deformed children figure in the stories of Clark Blaise, Mavis Gallant, Joyce Marshall, and newcomer Peter Behrens, while Norman Levine and Jack Ludwig emphasize the failure to continue a genealogical line.

When I embarked on my research project on English Montreal fiction, there was material available on a few of the better-known writers, but my chosen territory was otherwise uncharted. In addition to reading the fiction and such secondary material as I could find, I set about interviewing those I felt sure would be in the know, and these interviews all included the same question: "Who are the English writers of Quebec?"

Such an easy question, I thought at the outset. I soon learned otherwise. There were several people who found it unanswerable. "English?" they would repeat to me uncertainly, not sure I really meant English.

"Yes, English. Writers who write in English in Quebec."

There was no one who found it an easy question. "English writers in *Quebec?*" one woman said to me. "*Are* there any?"

There were scores of English writers working in Quebec at the time, almost all of them in Montreal, and they were almost entirely unknown even to professional readers, critics, and their peers. The reaction to my question was a revelation, and what it revealed was the invisibility of the writers. The woman who first said "*Are* there any?" was a Montrealer, and her response was typical of the people I interviewed both inside and outside of Quebec. In Toronto especially, my question elicited puzzlement, even disbelief. There was some interest there in Francophone Quebec writers. Not a whole lot of interest, but some, which went along with an assumption that Quebec writers are Francophones.

Hence the disbelief at my question. It had simply not occurred to most of the people I spoke to that there might be writers working in

English within Quebec. An entire generation of writers was unknown to the very people who had professional reasons to be familiar with them and their work.

When I gave a talk on my research findings at a conference of American specialists in Quebec Studies held in Quebec City, one of the American academics came up to me afterwards in a state of excitement. "What you are saying about Anglo Quebec writers," he marvelled, "is exactly what the Francophones were saying for years: that English Canada was paying them only token attention." In fact, the Anglos were even worse off, for English Canada had paid a token amount of attention to French Quebec; it was paying none at all to English Quebec. It saw no reason to do so.

I started compiling a bibliography based on what I knew and what I was learning, for the first step was to identify the writers and the works of fiction published in English since the war. I bought, borrowed, and read all the works by these authors that I could trace. I interviewed writers, publishers, academics, and reviewers within and outside of Quebec. It was basic research and it was great fun, because it forced me out into the world to meet librarians, booksellers, publishers, academics, reviewers, and the writers themselves.

"Well, there's Mordecai Richler...." That was the best most people could do in response to my key question. And that was not bad. Richler was a Quebec writer, he did write in English, and he had even moved back to Montreal. He was from an older generation — he had started publishing in the early 1950s — but I was interested in that older generation, too. Mentioning Richler was a decent start. If the same person had been able to rattle off two or three other names, as well, I would have called it a good response.

In a few cases, the people I spoke to withheld the names of writers they knew, and this is where my findings started taking me in a different direction, away from pure research and the printed page. Among the writers themselves, there were many who did know other names. They were close friends or members of the Writers' Union. One was a publisher who did not pass on the name of one of his authors.

So why did they not pass these names on to me? In the case of the publisher, it was a question of a contract dispute. The writers, for

their part, had more interesting reasons not to share information with me. Some of them simply didn't think much of their peers or of their work. And some wanted to keep me for themselves. They got so little recognition for their work as writers, the last thing they wanted was to share the limelight with anyone else. My first thought was to marvel at the idea that limelight might emanate from my research. My second was a realization of how desperate these writers must be for any kind of attention.

I was getting a glimpse into the complicated lives of writers. I was gaining insight into the situation of Montreal's English writers, and I was starting to suspect that their situation was extraordinary. Until this time, writing was something I had read as a critic, a scholar, and a teacher, something with no real existence aside from the printed page. I was now starting to understand how differently writing — one's own writing, the writing of other writers — looks to a writer. It was an education, in more ways than one. I was shocked that educated, literary people would impede the progress of research for more or less petty reasons. But I was fascinated, as well. I was dying to know more.

This was a time of extraordinary literary eccentricity, featuring several varieties of distancing. For a period of about six years a surprising number of the titles published by English Montreal writers were works of genre fiction or experimental fiction set in another world, in another time, in another moral landscape, in another language, or in some other kind of disconcerting narrative context.

These works include science fiction by Hugh MacLennan and Donald Kingsbury, dystopian satire by William Weintraub, historical fiction by Martin Kevan, crime fiction by Maurice Gagnon, romantic fiction by Donna Steinberg, comedies of Westmount manners by Edward O. Phillips, rambunctious surrealist hybrids (Trevor Ferguson, Ann Diamond, T.F. Rigelhof, and the George Szanto of *Sixteen Ways to Skin a Cat*), and other experimental fictions by poet and fiction writer Robert Allen and by Gail Scott, whose *Heroine* is the most daring novel of the period.

Published in 1987, *Heroine* is very much a contemporary Montreal novel written in English, and its structure — much of the eponymous heroine first-person story is told from her bathtub — appears to invite intimacy. Scott intentionally keeps

the reader at a distance, however, and the English-language reader at a great distance. Describing McGill students unflatteringly as "Waspies," with "little pea heads," the eponymous narrator comments, "Ugh, English Montreal,"[26] the novel is explicit in its alienation from English Montreal. The language of the novel includes not only a jump-cut style but a liberal use of French.

In Szanto's fine first novel *Not Working* (1982), a former cop from San Diego is displaced as a househusband in Wyoming, where he cannot resist investigating a suspicious death. This is a crime novel in which good characterization and a sure-handed treatment of a provincial social context help transcend the limitations of the genre. It makes a brief mention of Montreal, where Szanto was professor of Comparative Literature at McGill but, like so much other work produced in this period, it keeps the realities of contemporary Montreal at a distance.

There was mainstream work, as well, the most impressive titles of the period being Richler's *Joshua Then and Now* (1980) and *The Stories of Elizabeth Spencer* (1981) as well as Gallant's *Home Truths* (1981), which includes the Linnet Muir stories. These are writers whose international reputation had been made well before the decline of English Montreal. The prevalence of genre and experimental fiction produced by the younger Montreal writers during this period, however, suggests that many of them were feeling disconnected from the world in which they lived and uncertain of their place in that world.

Most literatures include genre fiction and experimental work, but it was unusual to find a literature so dominated by such writing. The predominance of marginal genres contributed to the greater marginalization of the writers in an English-Canadian literary context that was still anxious to establish its own respectability and international reputation with mainstream realist fiction. While the work of the writers I have mentioned was good and some of it brilliant, genre fiction is often commercial, and there was also, inevitably, ephemeral and inferior work that got published. This inferior work did not help the reputation of English writing from Montreal. Few English Montreal writers had been translated into French at the time, and those who had been published in French were even more marginal figures in the Francophone literary world than in English Canada.

One book that turned marginalization into its subject became a bestseller: Josh Freed's ruefully comic *Anglo Guide to Survival in Quebec* (1983), which focused on the absurdity of the situation of Anglos in the new Quebec. Freed and his co-author Jon Kalina and other contributors to this collection of short comic essays and gleeful cartoons (by *Gazette* cartoonist Terry Mosher aka Aislin) were journalists, not fiction writers, but humorous writing, too, is a marginal genre, so they had that much in common with other writers of the time.

One of the great qualities of the *Anglo Guide* is the gentleness of its humour at a time of hand-wringing and angst. Freed and his contributors did not take themselves or any of the rest of us too seriously, and the result was we also had to stop and laugh at ourselves. They had the audacity to broach the very topic that was on everyone's mind. With so many English Montreal writers doing everything at the time to avoid writing directly about Montreal and the situation in Quebec, the *Anglo Guide* created a readership for itself and made a spectacular success of an unlikely book.

I wrote reports on my work and published a number of articles, including "English-Quebec Fiction of the 1980s: A Case Study in Marginality," which was printed the U.S. journal *Québec Studies* and then reprinted in *Studies in Canadian Literature*. Many results of the three years I spent working on English fiction from Quebec, though, were not scholarly but practical, and they have informed much of the work I have chosen to do since as teacher, publisher, editor, literary translator, festival director, and writer. By the time I had finished my research, I had turned into an activist. Instead of merely reporting on the situation, I had set about trying to change it.

If you're a political activist and believe in the justice of your cause, your path is clear. Your problem is a political problem and it has a political solution. Throw enough publicity in, get enough people excited, and you're on your way. Hard to do, you may say. There are so few of us and so many of them.

That well may be. But what you are facing is simple in comparison with what well-intentioned literary types like me were facing in Montreal in the late 1980s. I was not the only one aware of the anomaly of the situation. There were others who believed

in the worth of English Quebec writing and who were aware of its invisibility. Some of the writers, certainly, were aware, as were two or three publishers, a few alert librarians, and a couple of booksellers; it added up to surprisingly few people at first. The numbers did start to swell when things got rolling.

Ours was about to become a literary cause, an aesthetic cause, an underground community cause and eventually, though we neither intended this nor wished it, a political cause. We didn't have money or large numbers of people. Literary causes don't usually have money, and if we'd had large numbers of people to marshal to the cause the problem would have been easily resolved.

There were not a lot of options in Montreal for writers looking for a publisher for a novel or a collection of short stories written in English in the early 1980s. Of the literary presses, the most significant was Véhicule Press, which started up as a publisher of poetry by the Vehicule poets[27] in the early 1970s and started including non-fiction in 1981. Vehicule poet Endre Farkas set up The Muses' Company in 1981 as a publisher of poetry. Antonio D'Alfonso's Guernica Editions was interested principally in Italian-Canadian as well as Francophone Quebec poets but did publish some fiction as well (Whiteman 1994). Houses regularly publishing fiction by English writers of Montreal in the 1980s were Jan and Gary Geddes's Quadrant Editions (1980-1983) and then Cormorant Books (from 1984), which published the short story anthologies out of Concordia University and some other fiction.

The balance starts shifting back to mainstream fiction in the second half of the decade. First novels appeared by Sharon Sparling (1985), Hélène Holden (1987), and David Homel (1988). Nuage Editions published its first four books in 1986, and its owner Karen Haughian has published fiction by English Montreal authors steadily ever since, changing the press's name to Signature Editions in 1999. In 1988 The Muses' Company published a fiction title — Kenneth Radu's *The Cost of Living* — that was nominated for a Governor General's Award. That was the year Simon Dardick invited me to edit a Fiction Series for Véhicule Press.

It was still slim pickings in comparison with Toronto, where not only small presses like Anansi and Coach House were thriving, but

McClelland & Stewart was billing itself as The Canadian Publisher and several international houses (Random House, Knopf, Penguin, HarperCollins, Macmillan) were actively seeking out Canadian talent but rarely choosing to publish fiction by English writers from Montreal. Most of these writers therefore missed out on the advantages of working with bigger houses, which are considerable and may include professional editing, publicity, international representation and rights sales as well as national distribution.

Toronto was humming not only with presses big and small, but also with literary magazines, bookstores, spanking new libraries, national print and broadcast media focusing on the new literary scene, readings series and now (from 1980) an International Festival of Authors at Harbourfront attracting writers from all over the world. It was also the base for the national writers', publishers', and magazine publishers' associations. When it came to writing in English in Canada, Toronto was at the centre and Montreal on the margin.

There was one heroic, marvellous bookseller in Montreal, Judith Mappin, who always took an active interest in stocking and promoting the work of Canadian writers — very much including local writers — in the now late and lamented Double Hook Book Shop. A couple of other booksellers — Richard King and Jonathan Penney at Paragraphe, John George at Argo, and Adrian and Luci King-Edwards at The Word — were supportive of local writers, stocked their work, and hosted book launches in their stores.

With few and notable exceptions, the English writers of Montreal were almost completely isolated both from French Quebec and from the rest of Canada. Toronto publishers did not often bother to send their writers to Montreal on tour, not convinced it would be worth their while. Even today, Toronto publishers will often omit Montreal from the itinerary of an international literary star; in the main, they keep the biggest stars to themselves in and around Toronto; if there is to be only one Canadian stop on a book tour, it will certainly be in Toronto.

It was hard to blame the publishers for bypassing Montreal in the 1970s and much of the 1980s. There was not much of a literary scene here, and what scene there was centred on meetings of members of the Writers' Union of Canada and social gatherings. There was a

little magazine called *Matrix* out in the Eastern Townships that was languishing with no more than 100 subscribers by 1988. *The Gazette* books section had an editor with no interest in the local literary scene; few of us had ever met her since she rarely attended book launches or any other literary events. We thought she published too many reviews of war memoirs and too few of books by Montreal writers.

The worst of it was that we didn't even have a very convincing case to make for English writers of Quebec. We had everything against us: the rival nationalisms that had squeezed us out, the demoralized state of English Montreal and its institutions, a sense of dereliction and alienation, a dearth of resources, and a terrible sense that we might just be out for the count. The clincher was the crushing suggestion that maybe the English writers of Montreal were just not very good.

This is the thought that lurks not too far in the background of all such situations. Women artists have always struggled with this, and lists of prize nominations often include only male writers, even today. This is bad enough; what is worse is that it is rare for anyone to even comment on the absence of women.

Writers from far-flung corners of Canada have always struggled with questions about the quality of their work, too, as have working class writers, aboriginal writers, Jewish writers, Arab writers, gay and lesbian writers, genre writers, Black writers, Italian-Canadian writers, writers from what was once the British Empire, not to mention writers from what was never the British Empire and who don't write in English. They've all been left off shortlists, too, and the reason always comes down to the same unanswerable argument: they're just not that good.

They're not that good, of course, until suddenly they're hot. It's impossible to convince a sceptic that a worthy writer is any good, but a writer who is hot will silence the sceptics. The writer who is hot just might be a woman of a certain age writing science fiction, which is the case of Margaret Atwood. It might be an Arab writer such as Rawi Hage working in English in Montreal. Once a writer is hot there is no further need to convince anyone that they are worth reading. The very same writer who was being ignored yesterday is on magazine covers and bestseller lists today. Suddenly, V.S. Naipaul has won the Nobel prize. Suddenly, Edeet Ravel publishes *Ten Thousand Lovers*. It's the

same writer, and sometimes it's the very same book, and while there will always be those who will say they're not very good, now it's the sceptics who go unheard.

"If a Montreal poet cannot get his work published outside of his own city, perhaps it is because his poetry is not that good." David O'Rourke, who published these words in the magazine *CVII* in 1980, is one of the few who actually went on the record questioning the quality of the work of Montreal's English writers (quoted in Norris 1993, 22). He was commenting on the poetry, but I heard the same thing about the fiction, and this doubting of the quality of Montreal's English-language writers is what lay behind the general lack of interest that I found everywhere among critics and commentators of the day.

It's virtually impossible to respond to this kind of put-down on one's own behalf. Championing other writers and their accomplishments has the advantage of not being self-serving, but it was not much more rewarding. Some of the work was inferior, but that can be expected of any body of work.

It plainly isn't enough to have a glorious history and a raft of published writers that some readers admire. It isn't enough to talk about how good this writer or that one is. I tried that, of course, and got pitying looks. I had to find some way to answer unanswerable criticisms.

The question of what is good is a question of value. It will include literary values — skill with characterization and a sense of structure, say — and it may also include non-literary values, some of which may be explicit and some of which will likely be unspoken. It may be that the reader is not wholly conscious of the fact that he can't stand novels written by self-important men or self-righteous women. Or that he is turned off by historical fiction. Or it may be that the reader is fully aware of these kinds of prejudices but prefers to pretend that his quarrel with the novel is a purely literary quarrel. Any number of factors can come into play, whether quietly or not, as a reader decides whether or not he will buy a particular book, whether or not he thinks the book he has just read is any good, whether or not he will recommend it to others. Is this going to be a book buried in what the

Spanish novelist Carlos Ruiz calls the Cemetery of Forgotten Books? Or is it going to be a book that people will be reading 20 or 100 years from now? If the reader happens to be a publisher or a reviewer with a wide audience, his influence will be that much greater, for better or for worse.

Which is all well and good, so long as we are all aware of what the judgment is based on. This is not always the case. If it were, there would be fewer geniuses like Herman Melville and Margaret Atwood who found it necessary to publish their own work. If we knew what literary judgments are based on, there would be fewer works of genius that sink into oblivion on first appearing, only — in just a few cases — to be rescued years or even centuries later.

Some of this process of selecting what is good and what is not good involves political values, and effective literary gatekeepers are always interested in work that seems apt for its political moment. A period of nation building will produce, as though on demand, works that can vie for the title of the great national novel. That was the case with *Two Solitudes* when it appeared in 1945. By the time that English Canada and Quebec were going their separate ways, however, the Toronto critics were denigrating MacLennan's accomplishment. MacLennan was not the man for the burgeoning CanLit scene of the late 1960s and early 1970s; he was part of the old guard, and Canada needed its critics to put him in his place and crown Margaret Atwood in his stead.

There are fashions in literature, as in much else, and sometimes the fashion will have something to do with the end of a war, the fall of the stock market, the rise of feminism, or a people's new sense of itself. These, in some measure, are what allow us to see the new fashion as beautiful.

And what creates a new fashion? That's where the solution lies: finding a way to create interest where there had been none. Being good is just not good enough. In the cutthroat world of literary reputations, you need a lot more than that. You need to be irresistible. Toronto will pay attention when there is something happening that Toronto needs to know about. For English Montreal writers, that eventually turned out to be international attention.

In the process of working on my research, I made several trips to Toronto, and I found these visits increasingly disheartening. There

were so many people there who were just not interested in English writers of Quebec, and I had learned it was impossible to convince the unconvinced.

The way that busy people judge how good you are is not only by reading your work and your reviews; it's also by the trophies you have to show off. You need prizes. You need to be an international star. You need impressive publications. You need big advances. You need to be a contender. You need to give busy people a reason why they should bother with you. And that means all the outward signs of success that go along with great writing.

The best revenge may indeed be writing well, but what to do when the very value of the writing is in doubt? English Montreal writing was not in fashion in the 1980s; that much was clear. The reasons it was not in fashion were less clear, which is why it was so difficult to respond to questions about the value of the writing. The best response was not to champion the writers — essential though that was; all writers need champions — but to create the conditions in which no one would doubt the value of their work.

English Montreal writers were powerless to change the priorities of the two nations that were so uninterested in us. Our best bet was to create the infrastructure and support networks that were missing. That takes time and volunteers. It has indeed been the job of many years and many hands, most of which belong to Montrealers and some of which belong to publishers, agents and critics in Toronto and elsewhere. We needed some of the talented writers who were already working — and others who were about to appear on the scene — to produce more good books. We needed them to be irresistible.

6
Making a Start

The English-speaking writers of Montreal had recovered their equilibrium sufficiently by the late 1980s to start thinking about how they could improve their situation, and the most urgent item of business was the creation of prizes to honour the best books published each year.

The idea for what would become the QSPELL prizes was first raised by poet and publisher Endre Farkas at a meeting of Alliance Quebec, which then brought bookseller Richard King and publisher Simon Dardick into the picture for some brainstorming (King 2009). A series of planning meetings followed, to which I was invited along with a dozen other members of the English-speaking literary world of Montreal. We came up with by-laws for a non-profit organization that would be called the Quebec Society for the Promotion of English-language Literature (QSPELL) and elected Richard King as president. Then we fixed a date in November 1988 for the first prize-giving gala, decided on the criteria, announced the procedure for submitting books, and set up juries for the best work of Fiction, Non-Fiction, and Poetry published in the previous year by a writer living in Quebec.

Alliance Quebec played a significant role in the creation of QSPELL, far bigger than some of us realized at the time. It was not clear, at least to me, that several of the individuals involved in the creation of QSPELL were also Alliance members or board members.

The awards might not have come into existence if it had not been for Alliance Quebec, so the literary milieu had reason to be grateful. Alliance Quebec also needed QSPELL, however, seeing QSPELL as a good way of increasing its appeal in the English-speaking community of Quebec, its membership, and its funding. Alliance Quebec was struggling for the hearts and minds of its Anglo constituency; at its height, a few years before QSPELL came into being, Alliance Quebec reportedly had some 40,000 members. Historian Graeme Decarie made the claim that it kept those names on the books even after its membership went into decline, as it soon did (Prosperi 1995, 59). Well-founded or not, such claims undermined the credibility of the organization and created the impression that it was fighting a losing battle, which soon turned out to be the case.[28]

Alliance Quebec was at this time a mild-mannered and respectable organization involving some of the brightest and best of English Quebec. Years later, it would end up on the "Angryphone" fringe until finally it lost the confidence of the federal government — and its funding — and ceased operations in 2005. Even in 1988, though, Alliance Quebec was political in a way that no cultural organization like QSPELL can afford to be political.

Alliance Quebec had been involved in the planning of the QSPELL awards from the beginning. We held some of our meetings in their boardroom, as well, which had created no difficulty in the months of planning. It was when the organization and the prizes became a reality that Alliance Quebec took on a much more visible role. This was problematical since Alliance Quebec had been spearheading successful challenges to some parts of Bill 101 and was regarded with hostility by Francophones determined not to change the Charter of the French Language on which so much of their identity and their future depended.

Alliance Quebec offered to send out invitations to the first awards, which were to be held in the Oval Room of the Ritz-Carlton Hotel. The QSPELL board agreed to this and was in fact grateful for the offer, since QSPELL was dependent on donations and had next to no resources. I suppose other members of the board — certainly those who were Alliance Quebec members — understood what it would mean for Alliance Quebec to mail the invitations. In my

naïveté, however, I thought Alliance Quebec — which was after all the beneficiary of substantial federal government funds — was just going to pay for the stamps as a contribution to the cause of QSPELL. I was therefore shocked the following week to receive in the mail my invitation to the inaugural awards in an envelope emblazoned with the Alliance Quebec logo.

Letting Alliance Quebec send out the mailing was a serious error. It meant that the best hope of the English Quebec literary world was politically compromised from the start. According to Richard King, Alliance Quebec also sent out fundraising letters on behalf of QSPELL (King 2009).

The other mistake QSPELL made was when one of the Alliance Quebec members on the board of directors proposed giving Peter Blaikie, the chairman of Alliance Quebec, a speaking role at the inaugural awards ceremony. By now aware of the negative impact that the too-close association with Alliance Quebec was having on QSPELL, I opposed this proposal. It was accepted, and I made a couple of phone calls, but no one seemed to want a battle on the eve of the great event. It is only now, from reading King's 2009 article, that I understand that others, too, were unhappy with the decision:

> The board invited the then chairman of the board of the Alliance Quebec to speak at the awards gala. The intent of this decision was to publicly acknowledge the help and support provided by Alliance Quebec. Of all the decisions we had made, this turned out to be the most controversial. More than one member of QSPELL complained that giving the podium to the AQ was tantamount to politicizing the awards and creating the risk of ghettoizing them.

This fear, King argues, was ill-founded: he insists that it "never turned out to be the case" that the awards were politicized or ghettoized. He stands by the board's decision to this day. "I thought then and still think now that it is totally appropriate to show gratitude to those people and institutions that helped launch the QSPELL awards" (King 2009).

King is right about showing gratitude, but I disagree with him about the political impact on QSPELL of the association with Alliance Quebec. This association alienated some English-speaking writers

and supporters from the start, and when we set up an honorary board and invited some prominent Francophones to join, they all declined, unwilling to put their names to an Anglo organization associated with Alliance Quebec.

The inaugural QSPELL ceremony took place in the lavish Oval Room of the Ritz-Carlton Hotel in November 1988. The room was swarming with writers, literary journalists, booksellers, publishers, librarians, academics, and sundry other book people — and also with some very well-dressed men who, I discovered, were among the top English-speaking lawyers in Montreal.

The chairman of Alliance Quebec stood up to speak, and he spoke well of the hopes we all had of QSPELL and made hardly a mention of Alliance Quebec. The unfortunate fact was, however, that QSPELL had made another public declaration that QSPELL was linked with Alliance Quebec.

There would be awards evenings to come, of course, over the next decade, long after the connection to Alliance Quebec had ended, but QSPELL never progressed beyond the awarding of prizes and was eventually superseded by the Quebec Writers' Federation. The emergence of QSPELL, politically compromised though it was, did have the effect of raising the profile of Anglo writers. The appointment of Mark Abley as Books Editor of *The Gazette* in 1987 was another improvement, since he was himself a writer with an interest in the literary scene and an awareness of the important role *The Gazette* could play. He woke *The Gazette* up to its role in the community, hired Montreal writers to write reviews of literary titles, and inaugurated a literary calendar of events.

Alliance Quebec, for its part, had hoped the link with QSPELL would have a positive effect on its own fortunes. As it turned out, the lobby group went into a tailspin within a few weeks of that November evening at the Ritz. On December 15, 1988, the Supreme Court of Canada ruled on the legal challenge to Bill 101 that Alliance Quebec had led. The ruling acknowledged that the prohibition of all other languages but French on public signs and posters and in commercial advertising was in opposition to freedom of expression.

Two weeks later, on December 31, 1988, the offices of Alliance Quebec in downtown Montreal were destroyed in a fire. The fire had been deliberately set, but no one claimed responsibility. Anglos suspected nationalist agitators, while some of the French-language press argued that Royal Orr, the president of Alliance Quebec, was himself the likeliest culprit. Orr sued, and the case was eventually settled out of court (Stevenson, 203).

The Commissioner of Official Languages, D'Iberville Fortier, said it appeared that the fire was intended to intimidate Alliance Quebec, and this was one of its effects. Its more general impact was on the already shell-shocked English-speaking community. With Alliance Quebec torched, there were going to be fewer Anglo Quebecers willing to play leadership roles. This left the field open to the real extremists who soon dominated Alliance Quebec, guaranteeing its increasing irrelevance and eventual demise.

There were several missteps in the 1980s and 1990s as Quebec Anglos lurched about in their sometimes ill-judged efforts to adjust to new realities. In spite of the mistakes made in its creation, QSPELL also gave us a taste of possibility. We now knew what it took to start up an organization, and we knew how important an organization could be. The accomplishment and the failings of QSPELL together inspired some of us to try again a few years later.

My own work on ways of increasing the writers' visibility was showing results. Geoff Hancock, editor of *Canadian Fiction Magazine*, asked me to guest-edit a special issue on English Quebec writing. This is to his great credit, not because he chose me, although I was happy that he did, but because he had the open-mindedness to give an English-speaking Quebecer a chance at a time when few CanLit gatekeepers were doing so. He was the first editor who showed me that it is possible to break in; you just have to do something to get yourself noticed.

It helped, too, that I was prepared to do a lot of work for no pay. It was my first editorial experience and I was neither surprised nor dismayed by the fact that the work was unpaid; I was fortunate to have a teaching position at John Abbott College and was years away from expecting financial compensation for my work in the literary milieu. I looked at editing the *CFM* issue as a valuable learning experience, and so it was.

The mandate Hancock gave me included a strict page limit and two rather long stories he himself wanted in the issue. Having met several writers whose work I thought highly of, I set about soliciting a short story from each. I thought that was what you did, and indeed there was nothing wrong with such a procedure, given the fact that I was working to a very tight deadline and — in these days before we had an organization of our own — there was no easy way of finding writers or communicating with them. I decided on criteria for inclusion and received more material than I could accept, given space limitations. I gave it all serious consideration, made my selection, wrote an introduction, and entitled the issue *Telling Differences: New English Fiction from Quebec*.

What I hadn't counted on was the writers' hunger for recognition. As word started to get around that I was editing a special issue of what was a very well-regarded and influential little magazine, I heard from a couple of writers who were incensed that they had not been invited to submit a story. I learned that writers' resentment has no bounds, and that the rage expressed by writers has no direct correlation to the justice of their case. I was also learning the depths of desperation felt by some of the English writers of Quebec.

Simon Dardick of Véhicule Press offered to reprint the magazine issue as a book and, when *Telling Differences* appeared in book form in the spring of 1989, it was reviewed prominently in both *The Gazette* (April 1, 1989) and in *The Globe and Mail* (May 6, 1989). The differences in the views expressed by the two reviewers are themselves telling, with the *Gazette* reviewer praising the book for the very quality the *Globe* reviewer objects to: the connection the book establishes between Montreal writers and the world in which they were living.

Robert Stewart, writing in *The Gazette*, admits to trepidation over the fact that this is a collection of stories by Montreal writers in English.

> Not only is there always a subliminal pressure to (unprofessionally) take it easy on the local heroes... but this is a special city going through a special period. Our poor old embattled Montreal Anglo culture can use all the stroking it can get.

"What a pleasure, then," he continues, "it is to report that *Telling Differences* is…a pleasure. No need for local boosterism here. These people can write." Stewart was himself an English-speaking Montrealer who knew first-hand what it was like to live and work here in English in the time of nationalism. What he appreciates most about the book is its connection to Montreal:

> The rap against much of the English-language fiction from Montreal in the past few years is that it was overly introspective, having little relevance to the situation of the people, especially the Anglos, living here. Editor Linda Leith says as much in the introduction. "During the later 1970s and into the 1980s very little English fiction was published in Quebec, and much of the work that did appear tended to shy away from any mention of contemporary realities." No such criticism can be made of such selections as Robyn Sarah's "New Management" or Kenneth Radu's "Real Men," which have the authentic ring of Montreal in the here-and-now.

The *Globe and Mail* reviewer Bonnie Burnard, in contrast, is ill at ease with the link between the writers and contemporary realities in *Telling Differences*. She opens with a lecture on the way that I establish a context for the stories:

> Linda Leith makes the implicit suggestion that it might be interesting to pay special attention to context when responding to the writing in this anthology. This suggestion is premature at best and a distraction if followed. Inclusion in an anthology does not necessarily qualify a piece of writing as literature, even if such inclusion is useful to academic discussion about larger literary issues. There should be a sharp distinction between the two questions: does this thing work (and why)?, and how does it compare to other work (from here and there, from now and before)? The question of context is best raised after broad critical response.

In a long review — it's wonderful today to see how much space newspapers once devoted to book reviews — she goes on to discuss each story in turn. Several of them (stories by Szanto, Lawrence, Radu, Rigelhof, Diamond, and Bereshko,) she singles out for high praise; the others interest her less. At the end, she comes back to her main point, which is to view the texts individually:

Telling Differences showcases literature, half a dozen pieces; they are interesting in themselves, for all kinds of reasons. Readers will recognize excellence, or the approach to it, as they read and they should be motivated to find the other books, the ones written by the most compelling writers in this anthology.

Viewing the collection from a vantage far from the world of English Montreal writing, Burnard is interested in individual writers and dismissive of context. Reviewing a collection of stories by people living through one of the most remarkable periods in Canadian history in Montreal, she acknowledges the quality of much of the writing but shows no interest in the world in which the writers were living.

Her own critical training may have steered her in the direction of the text and away from a link with the social context within which a writer works; that was certainly the norm in North American literary criticism at the time. It is not clear whether she would have had fewer reservations about a collection of work by Francophone Quebec writers — or English Canadians.

In the summer of 1988, two other opportunities came my way to work in the literary milieu. Simon Dardick invited me to edit the Véhicule Fiction Series, and the editors of the little magazine *Matrix* enquired if I might be interested in taking over the magazine.

Knowing of the difficulty some English writers in Quebec were having finding a publisher for their fiction, in the Véhicule Fiction Series over the following six years I chose to publish fiction by Quebec writers in English and some work by Jacques Poulin and Anne Dandurand in translation from the French. Many of the titles I selected and prepared for publication — works by Kenneth Radu, P. Scott Lawrence, Ann Diamond, George Szanto, Yeshim Ternar, and Robyn Sarah among them — were nominated for or won QSPELL Awards.

With *Matrix* magazine, I brought my colleagues Ken Radu and Diane Hibbard as well as designer Susan Valyi and others in to work with me on revamping the magazine. The point was to foster a readership for the work of English Montreal writers, and we succeeded in doing this by broadening the appeal of the magazine to include well-written and provocative essays on a wide range of cultural issues by talented Montreal writers. Maurie Alioff contributed a number

of articles on Canadian film, Henry Lehman on the opening of the Canadian Centre for Architecture, the sculpture garden, and the visual arts, Patrick Coleman on writers and writing, and Tom Ložar on the interface between Quebec and Canada, on the one hand, and Slovenia· and the former Yugoslavia on the other. The usual little magazine fare was included as well — poetry and short fiction selected from the mountains of submissions that came in from across the country — and a few works in translation, mostly from French, and some photography, graphics, and cartoons. Ken took responsibility for the poetry and book reviews, which were lively and opinionated; this allowed me to develop a hitherto unsuspected talent for selling ads to several of the publishers of books reviewed.

While I was publisher, circulation rose to about 2,000, which made *Matrix* the little magazine with the biggest circulation in all of Canada. When a long article about Canada's most successful literary magazines appeared in *The Globe and Mail* without even a mention of *Matrix*, I was disappointed but not surprised. Toronto was indifferent to what we were doing in Montreal.

The quality of *Matrix* was such that we substantially increased our funding from the Canada Council and obtained funding from the Conseil des arts de la Communauté urbaine de Montréal. One of the great frustrations was trying to persuade the Conseil des arts et des lettres du Québec (CALQ) to provide funding for what was at the time the only English-language cultural publication in Quebec. We applied repeatedly for funding for *Matrix* and we were turned down every time, appealed, complained, and got nowhere. The problem, we were told, was that there was no new money in the budget, and all the existing funding already went to existing publications, which was no doubt true, but it was also unsatisfactory. The magazine was an enormous amount of work and we could not afford to pay anyone other than the contributors, and that poorly. Eventually, in 1995, I told Radu and Hibbard I had had enough, and they decided they had, too.

I gave up *Matrix* because it was too much work to continue doing indefinitely for no pay — and because I had learned what I needed to learn from publishing and editing a literary magazine. In the same spirit in which the magazine had been offered to me in 1988, I offered it now to the creative writing people at Concordia University,

where Robert Allen was teaching. He edited *Matrix* for 20 years and, when he died in 2007, he left *Matrix* to poet and novelist Jon Paul Fiorentino, the current editor. *Matrix* finally started to receive CALQ funding after the handover.

My literary career moved up another notch in the summer of 1988 when Robert Lecker at ECW Press invited me to write a short study of Hugh MacLennan's novel *Two Solitudes* for a new series of monographs on "Canadian Writers and Their Works."

I had interviewed Hugh MacLennan a year or so earlier in the course of my research on English Montreal writers. He had lost his office at McGill by this time, and he resented the way he had been treated. He was shabby at this late stage in his career, and a bit querulous and forgetful when I met him in his office at Concordia. The novel he had published in 1945 was of considerable interest, however, and in writing about it for ECW Press, I researched its reception both at the time of publication and subsequently.

MacLennan was an old-fashioned character even in his own time: a student of the classics, a gentleman of the old school and in some ways an odd duck. While *Two Solitudes* is a failure in some ways, there are many supposedly great novels that don't stand up to scrutiny decades after publication. Rereading it would give me an opportunity to pay attention to the novel's vision of Canada. This is what I thought when I set about writing about *Two Solitudes* in English in the Montreal in 1988.

My reading of the novel — and of the commentary of earlier critics — turned out to be a revelation and, on hindsight, it seems to me inevitable that my take would be revisionist. English-Canadian critics had from the outset hailed the romance between Paul Tallard and Heather Methuen as symbolizing the union of English and French Canada. I disagreed. As a Montrealer alert to the sensitivities of Quebecers to an extent rare among English-Canadian critics, I pointed out that Paul Tallard is only half French. His mother was an English-speaking Irish Montrealer, and he himself was educated in English. And if Paul is half French, any children he and Heather might have would be only a quarter French.

It was impossible to have lived through recent Quebec history without being aware of the fears that Francophones had of assimilation

and of losing their language. When I read the English-Canadian critics' praise for the novel's union of French and English, therefore, I had a sense of discovery. Unlike these critics, who saw the value of the novel in its vision of Canada, I found that vision questionable. The symbolic meaning of the marriage between Paul and Heather should not, I argued, be viewed as the union of two great founding peoples. If it had symbolic meaning, its meaning was the assimilation of French Canada. I could see clearly why the novel had always been of such limited interest to Francophone readers.

By the time *Introducing Hugh MacLennan's Two Solitudes* came out in 1990, I was living in Budapest. I continued to edit *Matrix* magazine and manuscripts for Véhicule Press long-distance in the two years I spent there with my family. In the relative calm of Budapest, where I had no teaching responsibilities, I also wrote my first novel, *Birds of Passage*, which I brought back with me in August 1992. A new chapter was about to begin.

Late in the Afternoon

Political turbulence continued well into the 1990s with the Oka crisis in the summer of 1990 and ongoing wrangling over language and the constitution. Lucien Bouchard resigned from the federal cabinet in 1990 and formed a new federal political party, the Bloc Québécois, which was dedicated to independence for Quebec. In the federal election of 1993, when Liberal Jean Chrétien was elected prime minister of Canada, the Bloc won an extraordinary 49.3 per cent of the popular vote in Quebec and 54 of the 75 Quebec seats. Since the opposition vote in the rest of Canada was split between the Reform Party, the Progressive Conservative Party, and the New Democratic Party, the Bloc narrowly won the second largest number of seats in the House of Commons and became the official opposition. Jacques Parizeau led the Parti Québécois back to power in 1995, promising another referendum.

English writers in Quebec continued to languish. They had made a start, in the late 1980s, to improving their lot, but the results had been meagre. The Montreal writer Joel Yanofsky published a vivid account of the 1990 QSPELL Awards ceremony, in which he succeeds in creating the atmosphere of a dying world:

> The chandeliered Oval Room was elbow-to-elbow with the usual suspects, virtually the entire Anglo literary

community — writers, publishers, editors, critics, publicists, and even a few readers. (I realized that if a bomb dropped on the room, no one in Francophone Quebec — or in Toronto, for that matter — would notice.)… The fact is that if you're an English writer living in Montreal today, it's impossible not to feel like you've wandered into a production of Chekhov. Writing at the end of the 19th century, Chekhov dedicated himself to "taking the pulse of a dying world" and recording its "hour of sunset." And while the sun hasn't set here yet, it's certainly getting late in the afternoon.

For all our efforts, the situation in the literary milieu had barely improved. We were one of the poor cousins of Canadian literature, and it wasn't at all clear how we might fit into this new Quebec.

There were other poor cousins, certainly, in the CanLit scene. The competition was in fact stiff, with Black writers and Nova Scotians and any number of others jockeying for position as the worst treated of Canadian writers. Paradoxical as this may sound, it makes perfect sense. There is not a lot of glory for a writer in being just another neglected writer, or in being part of any group unjustly neglected by agents and editors, booksellers and media and the general reading public. There is some perverse glory in being the most neglected of all. That's when the great disadvantages under which you work can be properly recognized and you can assume the status of special victim.

Does it sound hard to take such claims seriously? It should, especially when you realize that it is difficult to find a writer anywhere who does not feel unjustly neglected. And especially when you consider the advantages that neglect confer on a writer.

For there are advantages. If you're convinced your work has been neglected just because you're an Anglo — or just because you were born in Greece — then it isn't your own fault that you've never made it. There is no weakness in your own work. The cards are stacked against you. You can blame it all on Margaret Atwood.

Every poor cousin has a case to make, and I have no wish to deprive writers of their consolations. I once listened to a talented young writer complain he was discriminated against because he was male and white, which he saw as handicapping him in the literary world.

He also happened to be a Montrealer, but he did not appear to view that as contributing to his lack of success. He had planned a reading with two other Montreal writers who were similarly handicapped and had billed the event as "Dead White Males." Women buy most of the books, he explained. Women are the readers. Women are the editors, too, in most cases, and the literary agents, and not infrequently the booksellers and librarians, too. They're all looking for the books they themselves like to read. I nodded slowly.

He had a case. Not a strong case — in comparison with women, who were often missing from awards shortlists — but a case. I heard a similar case expressed differently by a "dead white male" who was focused on the "white" rather than on the "males." His regret was that he was not South Asian or African.

The case of Montreal's Anglo writers is stronger than that of the Dead White Males because it's structural — built in to the kind of country we live in. It's also weakened by the very characteristic that defines it, which is the fact that we write in English.

This sounds like a conundrum, and there is something puzzling about it. There's something comical about it, as well; it's the kind of thing you might expect in an *Anglo Writers' Guide to Survival in Quebec*. And there's something serious here, too. Let me take it step by step.

Toronto did not have a lot of literary interest in Montreal writers working in French. These writers were not often published in English translation, and when their work did appear in English, it was seldom reviewed and little read. One of the great reasons that Quebec writers had for feeling resentment was, indeed, that they felt ignored in English Canada. In periods of crisis, however, Toronto did have a political interest in knowing what was going on in Quebec — and sometimes looked to Montreal writers for a sense of that.

Toronto had next to no interest in Montreal's Anglo writers. Toronto was busy asserting itself as the literary capital of English Canada, which meant outdoing Montreal and leaving Montreal's once-proud English-language literary tradition in the dust.

English-Canadian literature was emerging into the international spotlight in these years. The Booker Prize had been

created in 1970 to create an English award equivalent to France's *prix Goncourt*. Canadian writers were almost entirely absent from the shortlist until Robertson Davies's *What's Bred in the Bone* and Margaret Atwood's *The Handmaid's Tale* were shortlisted in 1986. In the decade that followed, it was rare for a Canadian work *not* to appear on the shortlist. Mordecai Richler's *Solomon Gursky Was Here* was shortlisted in 1990 and Rohinton Mistry's *Such a Long Journey* in 1991 and for *A Fine Balance* in 1996. Richler, who had been passed over by the jury for the Governor General's Award, was the only English Montreal writer whose name appeared on the Booker shortlist in these years.

Atwood's *Cat's Eye* was shortlisted for the Booker in 1989, *Alias Grace* in 1996, and Atwood won the Booker in 2000 for *The Blind Assassin*. Michael Ondaatje's *The English Patient* won the Booker in 1992 with Barry Unsworth; Carol Shields's *The Stone Diaries* was nominated in 1993.

The other major English-language prize for fiction is the more recent International IMPAC Dublin Literary Award, created in 1996. In its first year, Jane Urquhart's *Away* and Mistry's *A Fine Balance* were both shortlisted (1996); Atwood (*Alias Grace*) and Guy Vanderhaeghe (*The Englishman's Boy*) followed in 1998; and Alistair MacLeod won in 2001 for *No Great Mischief*.

French-speaking Montreal had long been focused on its own writers and had little interest in any Canadian writing in English; its interest in English Montreal writing was even more limited. There were a few Francophone academics, publishers, and translators who had a professional interest in our work. The fact that we write in English matters little to most *Québécois*. If I met with bewilderment from English-speaking literary types in the late 1980s, I met with incredulity from most Francophones, who simply never imagined there might be writers working in English in Montreal. This ignorance was understandable, for there were few books by English Montreal writers being translated into French and published in Quebec, and it was rare for French-language publications to review work in English.

We were therefore even more invisible to Francophone readers than we were to Anglophones. The fact that we write in English was

about as advantageous to us as writing in Russian is to a contemporary British writer; in other words, it was not at all advantageous. It is hard to imagine a less advantageous position for a writer to be in. And yet, invisible though we might be, we were still Anglos, after all, and there were many people in Quebec and outside it who persisted in considering English-speaking Quebecers dominant, as though nothing had changed. As though we were not, in fact, a shrinking and politically ineffectual minority. As though we were making it all up when we protested, as some of us have occasionally done.

Even today, English is still seen by many as the language of the oppressor here in Montreal, the language associated with Anglos who refused to speak French and were less than respectful to the language and culture of the majority. There was a danger in the 1960s and 1970s that the French culture of Quebec would disappear in the great ocean of English across North America. English is the lingua franca of the contemporary world, so spectacularly successful worldwide as to threaten more fragile languages, including Quebec French. It was necessary for measures to be taken to protect the French language and culture.

I wasn't here in the bad old days. Neither I nor any other writer working here nowadays had anything to do with oppressing French-speaking Montrealers. I would never deny the global power of English, but I'm certainly not to blame for it. I write in English, and English is still feared and despised by some Francophones. This is why some English Montreal writers keep their heads down and stay out of the way.

Anglos are a minority within a minority, living in a city in which everyone is a member of one minority or another. There are Anglophones who show no more interest in Quebec radio, television, film, and writing than Francophones show in Anglophone culture, and there are cultured Anglophones far more interested in Francophone than in Anglophone culture, too. Most English writers here are on the margins of the English-speaking minority, and there are two or three who see themselves as being on the fringe of that already marginal fringe.[29] The global success of the English language, which might have been such a boon to those of us who write in English in Montreal, has not only been a boon. It has complicated our lives. We would have been better off writing in French, especially since we are fortunate enough to live in a great French-speaking city.

In the years since the Quiet Revolution, the English writers of Montreal had disappeared into the cracks between Canada and Quebec. Our neglect, though not necessarily deeper or more damaging than that of other poor cousins, is uniquely connected with the fissure between these rival nationalisms.

The Quebec side of the story is complicated by the link between nationalism and the French language, and also by a persistent state of alarm among the Francophone majority of Quebec over the power of the English language and the fragility of French. English is the language of historic oppression, here in Quebec, and the French language, always important, became the cornerstone of Quebec's identity after the decline of the Church in the 1960s. To be a Quebec writer meant writing in French. The very definition of Quebec literature therefore excluded us, as I discovered at a colloquium I participated in at the Université de Montréal in 1997.

The colloquium had been organized by writer and scholar Pierre Nepveu, who had a rare understanding that the role of Quebec's English-language writers did need to be thought through.[30] In my remarks at the colloquium, I described myself as an English-Quebec writer — une écrivaine anglo-québécoise. However, the keynote speaker, the distinguished literary critic Gilles Marcotte, argued that, by definition, there could be no such thing as an English-Quebec writer (1998/1999). English-speaking Quebec had not only become a non-place; I had become a non-person living in this non-place.

I was, in fact, not only a non-person living in a non-place. I was a non-person living in a non-place and writing in the most powerful language on the planet.

Some victims we turned out to be. The poor little English writers of Montreal? Can we be serious? Montreal's Francophone writers have certainly had their own successes, and some of them, too, were born elsewhere. As I write, Dany Laferrière, Jean Barbe, Edem Awumey, Kim Thuy, and Catherine Mavrikakis are nominated for prestigious French prizes — the French equivalent of the Booker, the IMPAC Dublin, and the Costa prizes. But Quebec writing is overshadowed by writing from France, and the Francophone writers of Montreal await the sustained level of international recognition that literary Toronto has now been basking in for decades.

From most points of view, in other words, those of us who write here in English look like a pretty privileged lot, and no one was going to waste a lot of time feeling sorry for us. Writing in English was the reason for our neglect, and writing in English was the reason why we have no right to feel neglected.

One of the most frustrating things for some of us Anglo Montreal writers was that the one who got all the attention was Mordecai Richler. The success of CanLit might have outstripped that of Francophone Quebec writing, but Quebec had its own star system. Anglo Quebec writers were almost without exception shut out, and it was no consolation that the exception was Mordecai Richler. He was undoubtedly a star, even if he was the star Quebecers loved to hate. He was not only in a different literary class entirely from the rest of us; he was of a different generation. That was a question of attitude as well as age.

Beloved as he clearly was by his family and friends, Richler was abrasive in public. He had created an uproar in Quebec with his scathing attack on the language laws in the pages of *The New Yorker*, which I read in Budapest in 1991, and which was published in book form as *Oh Canada! Oh Quebec! Requiem for a Divided Country* in 1992. Most of what he had to say was perfectly accurate, which didn't help. The situation was so ludicrous that there was little need for him to exaggerate for comic effect. The passage that follows is accurate in every particular:

> Consider the hard lot of your beleaguered good neighbors to the north, Quebec's English-speaking — and English-writing — minority. Our mother tongue is an affront to the province's *visage linguistique*. Following the introduction of the French Language Charter in 1977, our supermarkets and department stores lost their compromising apostrophes. Eaton's, for instance, was born again as Eaton. In the absence of the Keystone Kops, the language police — or tongue troopers — came into play, searching for sign offenders. Pondering the corruption of the language of Racine and Voltaire, alert Québécois lexicographers rendered the humble "hamburger" edible by renaming it the *hambourgeois*. Road signs that read ARRÊT/STOP were uprooted, displaced by politically

correct signs that read ARRÊT only. Grieving English-speaking Quebecers, in quest of signs that still read STOP, had to travel to France.

Francophone Quebecers were offended by Richler's account of the language law they held so dear. They were especially offended by the fact that he had mocked Quebec in the pages of a prestigious American publication. There is something poignant about this. When French-speaking Quebec artists and intellectuals gave up on the possibility of recognition from English Canada, they looked instead for international recognition. Now here was Richler giving them a dressing-down in a prestigious U.S. magazine with an international readership. He was punished with a very public lashing in the Francophone media, which added to the reasons other Anglo writers had to keep their own heads down.

Why have Anglos generally been so unwilling to speak up? If there are injustices apparent to English Montreal writers, what has stopped them from taking their case to a public forum? This is a good question. Part of the answer is likely fear, since the few who have spoken out — Richler being the best example — have been vilified. Some of us who took action in order to provide a forum for Montreal's English writers have come in for criticism and ostracism. The criticisms of the Quebec film industry expressed by Montreal filmmaker Jacob Tierney are a recent example of what happens to those who speak out (Bérubé 2010, McPherson 2010). Tierney, who described the Quebec film world as being "*blanc blanc blanc,*" is fluent in French; another reason some Anglos are reluctant to speak up is the thought of having to defend their position in the Francophone media.

I was of two minds about Richler. There is something exhilarating about a writer who has the guts to come right out and tell it as he sees it, especially when he does so as comically as Richler. He certainly didn't lack courage, though even he might have been taken aback by the backlash his attack provoked from Quebec commentators of all stripes. And yes, he was picking on Quebec in this particular book, but he didn't pick on Quebec particularly. He had taken on other targets in the past, including English-Canadians and Jewish Montrealers, and had enemies long before he took on

Quebec nationalists. We don't expect a satirist to be fair-minded and tactful anyway; that isn't part of his job description. We don't want a satirist to pull his punches.

If I admired Richler's courage, I had reservations, as well. Accurate as he was in much of what he wrote, Richler was a throwback and an extremist, waving a red rag at the bull of Quebec. The fact that he didn't speak French was an embarrassment to us if not to him. There was something intolerant about Richler's polemic, which served to reinforce old stereotypes of the Anglo-Quebecer who lacks understanding of Quebec and sympathy for its aspirations. In the charged atmosphere of the time, it didn't help us younger writers at all that the most prominent Anglo writer was so blazingly anti-Quebec. Whatever we were, we were not going to follow in Richler's footsteps. We were going to define ourselves differently. Much as we might admire Richler, we were going to distance ourselves from him.

I returned to Montreal from Hungary in August 1992 and picked up my John Abbott teaching job where I had left off. A few writers and publishers had gathered to talk about the need for more adequate organizations. The publishers, Endre Farkas of The Muses' Company and Karen Haughian of Nuage Editions (now Signature Editions), were both active in the fledgling English-language publishers' association. The writers involved were Peter McFarlane, Sharon H. Nelson, and Elias Letelier-Ruz, none of whom I had met. Within a week of my arrival home, Nelson had called to invite me to a meeting. Another person invited was Guy Rodgers, who headed up the Quebec Drama Federation.

I threw my lot in with this little gang without knowing what I was getting into. Guy did, too. It was a bumpy ride, in the course of which we managed to alienate both the Writers' Union of Canada (TWUC) and QSPELL and many of their Montreal members.

Things started to go wrong when McFarlane — Guy took to calling him "snarlin' McFarlane" — made a statement critical of TWUC that was gleefully reported in the cultural weekly *The Mirror*. The small writing community split into two factions: those of us who wanted a new organization, and the more conservative (and more numerous) literary types who thought we already had what we needed in the Writers' Union of Canada and QSPELL.

Organizations are not on their own creative, but good arts organizations are essential for creativity to flourish. One of the great strengths of the CanLit scene in Toronto was precisely that time, thought, and effort had gone into creating the organizations needed for lift-off: the literary magazines, the publishing houses, the writers' organizations, the professional associations, the readings series, a literary festival, and all the rest. The same kind of infrastructure had been built within Quebec to support writing and publishing in French. The key weakness of the Anglo literary scene in Quebec was the lack of a supportive infrastructure.

The organizations we writers had in 1992 were simply not up to the job. The Writers' Union of Canada would never be much help to us, based as it was in Toronto and in significant ways indifferent to English Montreal; this didn't stop us trying, over the next few years, to get the Union to respond to what we needed. Our demands, which came to the notice of the membership only when McFarlane was briefly chair of the Writers' Union of Canada in 1998, included electronic ballots for members unable to attend the annual general meeting, moving the office from Toronto to Ottawa, and increased lobbying on behalf of writers.

QSPELL was our own Quebec organization. The QSPELL prizes were starting to have an impact, but the organization had never progressed beyond the Ritz and its annual book awards. If we needed a better organization within Quebec, why didn't we just reform QSPELL?

This might have been an option with a different cast of characters. There were a few difficulties, however. One was that QSPELL was not interested. With stolid opposition from the QSPELL board of directors, it turned out to be easier to start a different organization altogether. For QSPELL had become ossified in its few years of existence. As writers, we needed QSPELL to become active in ways other than the prizes alone, and we were frustrated when our suggestions were brushed aside. I suspect the reason was a lack of time, energy, and resources, but to a few of us on the outside, the complete disregard of such suggestions had an arrogant air. Peter McFarlane and another writer, Linda Ghan, got themselves elected to the board of directors of QSPELL, where they soon had the effect of alienating other members. Things were heating up.

Another problem was that QSPELL's mandate was limited. It was not a writers' organization, and it looked unlikely that it could be remade into one. There were going to be battles either way, because there were entrenched interests both in QSPELL and at the Writers' Union of Canada that simply saw no need for change. The battles would in all likelihood have been even bloodier if we had attempted to take over QSPELL.

The organization we really needed was the one we did eventually create: the Quebec Writers' Federation (QWF), which came into being in 1998. In 1992, we were two steps away from that. The creation of the Federation of English-language Writers of Quebec or FEWQ was the first step, and I doubt that QWF would ever have come into being if it had not been for FEWQ, even if this was an unfortunate name that could be pronounced in one of two comically problematical ways — as "few-cue" and as "fuke," to rhyme with puke. That caused a certain amount of merriment, and the organization itself created a stir.

We faced many challenges in our attempt to set up FEWQ, for we did not have any funding at the outset and we faced a general lack of interest from the world at large as well as opposition from those involved in existing organizations. We knew there would be battles to fight. As it turned out, the toughest of these battles were with other writers. Guy Rodgers was elected president of FEWQ in 1993, and I became vice-president.

We would not have won the day if it had not been for the funding that we succeeded in getting from the Quebec government almost as soon as the new organization was incorporated. This was funding for which we had the publishers Karen Haughian and Endre Farkas to thank, for they had been lobbying the Conseil des arts et des lettres du Québec (CALQ) on behalf of the English-language community. It was also funding for which QSPELL was not eligible, not being a writers' organization. The three organizations that benefited were the Federation of English-language Writers of Quebec, Quebec Drama Federation, and the Association of English Publishers of Quebec (now known as the Association of English-language Publishers of Quebec, or AELAQ).

QSPELL was smarting at this point, but we put out preliminary feelers about a possible merger with FEWQ that was the second step leading to the 1998 creation of the Quebec Writers' Federation.

My first novel, *Birds of Passage*, was published in the spring of 1993 and launched at the book fair organized at Le Faubourg Ste. Catherine by the publishers' association. *The Tragedy Queen*, my second novel, was published two years later, when my publisher sent me on what was billed as the Quanglo Tour of Quebec Anglo writers. The writers included in the tour were fiction writers Edeet Ravel and Julie Keith, poets Ian Stephens and Mark Abley, and non-fiction writer Joe Fiorito. We were received on Parliament Hill by Secretary of State Sheila Finestone and in the Bureau du Québec à Toronto by the cultural attachée Fabienne Bilodeau. We got good press, too, both in Montreal, where *The Gazette* put us on the front page, and in each city we visited. It was a time when Quebec was very much in the news, for Jacques Parizeau, now premier, was planning the second referendum for October 1995. That referendum would be both bitter and divisive — and it would inspire me and some of my writer friends with a wish to build bridges between Anglophones and Francophones.

8
Ferment

The referendum question guaranteed that if the people of Quebec voted for independence, Quebec would offer a partnership with the rest of Canada before declaring sovereignty.[31] Whatever reassurance that clause represented to anxious voters was dashed when journalist Chantal Hébert broke the story in *La Presse* that this guarantee was a sham. In a June 13 meeting with 15 foreign diplomats, she reported, Parizeau had stated that what mattered most was to get a majority vote from Quebec citizens for the proposal to secede from Canada. Once they had voted "Yes," he reportedly said, Quebecers would be trapped like lobsters in boiling water: "*comme des homards dans l'eau bouillante.*"

This was a cartoonist's delight, but the Referendum turned out to be a near-death experience for Canada. There can be no better visual representation of the rival nationalisms of Canada and Quebec than the gigantic rival flags displayed in Montreal that October. The vote was hair-splittingly close: 49.42 per cent for sovereignty vs. 50.58 per cent against. Federalists protested that ballots had not been counted properly; sovereignists, angry in defeat, claimed that the federal government spent far more on its campaign than was legally allowed. The Referendum left a legacy of shock on the one side and rage on the other; about the only thing shared by the two camps was distrust of the other.

It was in this atmosphere that, on February 12, 1996, publisher of the influential daily newspaper *Le Devoir*, Lise Bissonnette, wrote about Anglophone artists and intellectuals engaging with Quebec. Everywhere in Montreal, she wrote, in galleries and museums, Anglo Quebec musicians and performing artists, writers and translators feel close to Quebec as it is and especially as it could be if they had a bigger role to play.

No editorial has ever hit home as much as this one. No editorial has ever seemed more timely.[32] When I read it, I felt as though it spoke directly to me, and that it spoke to what I was doing at that very time. For it was in that same atmosphere that Ann Charney, Mary Soderstrom, and I paid a visit to the Union des écrivaines et des écrivains québécois and played out the exact kind of engagement Bissonnette described in her editorial.

Interaction between English-speaking and French-speaking writers was not unheard of, but it had been very limited. The English Montreal writers with the most interaction with the Francophone milieu were lesbian feminists like Gail Scott and Erin Mouré, whose network was not only with Francophone feminists within Quebec but also with English-Canadian women. These writers had their own publications (*La Nouvelle Barre du jour*, *Spirale*, *Tessera*), publishing houses (Remue-ménage, Press Gang, Women's Press, and others), and literary translators such as Susanne de Lotbinière-Harwood and Barbara Godard. Many of the writers doubled as editors, anthologists, critics, and theoreticians with university posts, so that university courses and postgraduate theses were devoted to their work both then and since.

The feminists had, in other words, put in place the kind of infrastructure and support that other English-language writers of Montreal lacked. If Toronto provided one example to us of how to create the context within which writers could thrive, Montreal feminists provided another; given their bilingualism and their alternative stance to mainstream CanLit, their example was in several ways the more relevant to the situation of English-language writers within Quebec.

These feminists writing in English in Montreal had succeeded in turning the peculiarities of their situation to their advantage. If we

felt as though we were without a country, they had created their own principality. As lesbians, they too felt excluded, but where some of us felt rejected by both English Canada and Quebec, they had managed to gain acceptance by a receptive readership in each. If they, too, felt they were on the margins, they had turned unfashionable marginality into the cool alternative of transgression. If we were struggling to emerge out of a catastrophic decline, they were riding the great wave of feminist scholarship of the 1970s and 1980s.

They had no need for English-speaking Montreal, which was still floundering in an unfashionable urban wilderness. They might even have had a need to keep us at a distance. Partly this was the distance that fashionistas keep from the down-at-heel; partly it was the exclusivity that any group needs as it defines itself as an alternative. It was also more than that, for literary fashions, especially in Quebec, are also political decisions.

Even if Gail Scott viewed Anglo-Montrealers with distaste and wanted little to do with us, I thought her a remarkable example to English Montreal writers. She had been living in the *Quartier latin* for years, where I for one was only just now taking my first steps across town to the Maison des écrivains. She was experimental in her work, where most of the rest of us were writing the kind of old-fashioned realist fiction — or worse, genre fiction — she could not see the point of writing (Leith 1987). She was politically radical, where some of us were saddled with old Anglo baggage that didn't even belong to us.

Gail Scott and Erin Mouré were gaining recognition for their work outside the feminist fold. Nominated three times for the Governor General's Award, Mouré won in 1988 for *Furious*; she has gone on to have one of the most distinguished careers of all contemporary English-Canadian poets. Scott's *Heroine* was nominated for the very first QSPELL fiction award in 1988, and Mouré won in 1989 for *WSW*. The feminists were also assertive, where we were tentative, and in their solidarity, they had created what Gail Scott described to me as "a safe place to write."

Charney, Soderstrom, and I were ourselves pioneers, ahead of most of Montreal's English-language writers in our interest in and openness to the Francophone literary milieu. QSPELL had

relinquished its ties to Alliance Quebec, and most writers, like the remaining English-speaking population in general, had made their peace with the new Quebec, but it was rare for any to forge links with Francophone writers.

I was the Quebec representative on the National Council of the Writers' Union of Canada that year and would be elected 2nd vice-chairperson in the summer of 1996; Charney and Soderstrom were members of the Writers' Union, Charney and I were members of UNEQ, and we were all members of the board of the Federation of English-language Writers of Quebec, as well. As writers active on behalf of English writers of Montreal, the three of us were the vanguard.

Charney had been published in French and had close ties to the Francophone scene through friendships formed in her postgraduate studies in the McGill French department and through connections developed through her coverage of Quebec politics and culture in *Maclean's* and *Saturday Night*; some of her essays were collected in *Defiance in Their Eyes*. Soderstrom was a transplanted American fiction writer and journalist who had moved to Montreal with her husband, a McGill professor; in the mid-1990s she was at the beginning of a productive period of writing that would result in four novels, a collection of short fiction, and two works of non-fiction over the next ten years.

Ray Filip and Endre Farkas had some ties to the Francophone literary milieu, and had organized readings with writers working in both languages. Translator David Homel, who had recently published his first novel *Electrical Storms*, was connected with the Francophone writers and publishers not only because of his work as a translator but also because he covered the Quebec publishing scene for the English-Canadian book trade publication *Quill & Quire*, a position later assumed by Soderstrom. Yann Martel, a newcomer to the scene with a collection of short fiction, *The Facts Behind the Helsinki Roccamatios* in 1993 and a first novel, *Self*, in 1996, is a Francophone who had been educated in English and who chose to write in English.

It was on an afternoon late in 1995 that Charney, Soderstrom, and I set off to propose a historic event to UNEQ: an event in French and in English that would be the first-ever collaboration between

the two national writers' unions on an event featuring some of the members of each organization.

The Maison des écrivains, the building in which UNEQ has its offices, is a greystone on avenue Laval, a few doors from Carré St-Louis. It had once belonged to Claude Jutra, the distinguished filmmaker whose Alzheimer's disease and eventual suicide had been the subject of an article Charney had written in *Saturday Night*. I was impressed by that and by the fact that she knew the gentleman who was leaving the building as we arrived, a literary journalist well known in Francophone circles. I myself had never heard of Jean Fugère before that day.

I had read and reviewed books in French by Quebec writers. I had published translations of some of their work both in *Matrix* and in the Véhicule Fiction Series. I had written a book about *Two Solitudes* that was sympathetic to Francophones' concerns about assimilation by English Canada. None of this had prepared me for the Maison des écrivains, which was foreign territory for me in 1998.

My French, though correct, was more literary than social. My husband and I had sent our sons to French schools, but we did not otherwise do much mingling in the Francophone world, partly because he was less at ease in French and partly because we had both taught — he at Concordia University and I at John Abbott College — in English institutions with English-speaking students and colleagues. Charney and Soderstrom were part of a future I was just starting to glimpse. They both seemed far more at home than I was in this appealing wider Montreal world. I was excited to venture into this world, unsure of myself, but also determined.

The employee we met turned out to be a junior. UNEQ had not seen fit to have the *directeur général* receive us, let alone the writers who were members of the board of directors. The young woman was well-intentioned and slightly officious. She listened to us, asked a few questions, took notes, and hesitated. She would get back to us. It was a less than enthusiastic response to what we had thought a momentous overture.

We persisted, and she called to ask us to return with a budget for the event we were proposing. We struggled to put a budget together in French. My two companions, whose French was more practised

than mine, had little experience of financial statements. I had worked with budgets on *Matrix* grant applications, but I had done that in English; I found it daunting to find the right vocabulary in French. When we all headed over to the Maison des écrivains again, early in 1996, our young woman, Nicole Blouin, suggested we might need a "*commanditaire*"; my companions nodded thoughtfully. I had no idea what she meant until eventually the context of the discussion taught me that Blouin was talking about a sponsor.

I have worked in French most of the time in the intervening years. Putting a budget together in French presents no challenge for me now. But working in French was not always *évident*, to use a word that does not have an exact English equivalent, certainly not to me, and the vocabulary of financial statements was a stretch for Charney and Soderstrom, too. Neither the Writers' Union of Canada nor UNEQ offered assistance.

At least one lesson took us all by surprise. That was that we must not, under any circumstances, refer to the event we had in mind as a "bilingual" event. Blouin was stern with us about this. "Bilingual" pressed all the wrong buttons in the political minefield of Quebec, associated as bilingualism was with Frank Scott, the Royal Commission on Bilingualism and Biculturalism, Pierre Elliott Trudeau, and the federal Liberal Party. She suggested that we describe our event as taking place "in two languages" or "in French and English" instead. We nodded meekly and complied. I had thought of our venture as a literary event with some welcome bridge-building; I had not realized how much political meaning it had.

We were warming to our task. Over the weeks and months that followed, we sorted out the budget to Blouin's satisfaction and doubtless that of the superiors to whom she was reporting every step of the way. We planned a date for the event. We decided on the venue, wrote out and shared proposals, and brainstormed about a good name for our event that would include both languages. Blouin was the one who came up with "Write pour écrire."

We prepared an application for funding from the Conseil des Arts et des lettres du Québec, finalizing it in the nick of time for an imminent deadline. And our proposal was so daring and original that in due course we did get the funding requested. The funds went into a bank account that Charney and I — who lived near to each

other — had opened in our neighbourhood in our personal names for this purpose: UNEQ did not wish the application to go in under its name or the funding in its bank account, and the Writers' Union of Canada, based as it was in Toronto, was ineligible to accept funding from a Quebec government agency.

We agonized over who the Anglo participants would be. I thought we should invite Mordecai Richler, but Charney and Soderstrom were adamant that we not invite him since he was *persona non grata* among Francophones. I was outnumbered, so we never got to find out how UNEQ would have reacted to the idea of inviting him. The criteria we finally agreed to were that the writers chosen should be able to speak French and — since the writers would be reading excerpts from one another's work in translation — have at least one book that had been published in French translation.

The criteria for Francophone writers were different. While we limited our choice to writers who had had a book translated into English, we did not expect the Francophones to be fluent in English. At our event, the burden of bilingualism would be on the Anglos, even if we kept the word "bilingualism" to ourselves. Blouin let us know the Francophone writers chosen by UNEQ — we were aware that there were invisible forces lined up behind her. At her suggestion we hired spoken word artist D. Kimm as artistic director of the event.

Write pour écrire took place at the Lion d'or on October 31, 1996. The English-language writers were Yann Martel, Josh Freed, Gail Scott, and Ann Charney, and the Francophones were Monique Proulx, François Charron, Nicole Brossard and José Acquelin. The host for the evening was the impeccably bilingual Winston McQuade — or rather, the host was Winston McQuade, who spoke French and English equally well.

We had to turn people away, the evening was so popular, more like a happening than a literary event. What was taking place on stage was one thing, Francophone writers reading in French the work of Anglophone writers in translation, and vice versa, with music and performance. Off-stage was at least as interesting, so many Francophones, so many Anglophones, various Allophones, all mingling with one another and amazed to find themselves in the same room.

Bruno Roy, the president of UNEQ, showed up for the occasion — this was the first time I had ever seen him, in all the months of planning. The public in the Lion d'or that Hallowe'en night was about half French-speaking and half English-speaking, which was itself remarkable and a first for any significant literary event in Montreal. This was the first time that the two national writers unions, the Writers' Union of Canada and UNEQ, had collaborated on a literary event with the participation of members of both organizations, although the Writers' Union of Canada had had almost nothing to do with it, really; it was more a collaboration between three Montreal English-language writers and UNEQ, even if UNEQ kept in the shadows for most of the process.

Most remarkable of all was that these Francophones and Anglophones were sharing the same space and celebrating the same writers in French and English. The timing was important, too, a little more than a year after the bitterly divisive referendum. We all looked around the room, marvelling at the audience as much as at the show itself. I myself found the evening inspiring. It showed there was an audience in Montreal for events that crossed the old divisions.

A year or two before this, UNEQ had created a Festival de la littérature, which showcased Francophone writers, mostly from Quebec, in a series of literary events in French. Greatly encouraged by the success of Write pour écrire, later that fall of 1996, we went back to the Maison des écrivains to propose that UNEQ invite some Anglo writers to participate in its festival. This did not seem to us a radical suggestion; we did not suggest they include events or readings in English. To make it easy for them, I prepared a bibliography of works by English writers of Quebec who had been translated and whose French was sufficiently good to allow them to participate on stage in French. It was a long list. Nothing came of this, which disappointed us; the next edition of the Festival de la littérature came and went in the spring of 1997 without any greater openness to English writers than before.

If Anglo writers were to appear at a literary festival in Montreal, it was now clear that it would not be at the Festival de la littérature. This realization was the beginning of the idea for an international literary festival that would include English as well as French.

First, though, we turned our attention to a merger between QSPELL and the upstart Federation of English-language Writers of Quebec.

There was considerable opposition to the merger from old-guard QSPELL members and board members who viewed FEWQ with suspicion and, with some justification, saw the merger as a FEWQ takeover. One of the main battlegrounds was over the name of the new organization that would be formed by the merger of QSPELL and FEWQ. Those who finally warmed to the idea of fusing the two organizations were insistent that the new organization keep the name QSPELL. Those of us who had been involved in FEWQ were adamant that we needed to change the name. None of us had any wish to perpetuate the ridiculous name of FEWQ.

There were strong arguments for and against changing the name of QSPELL. QSPELL had by this time a track record — and name recognition — going back ten years, its loyalists said. The QSPELL name was known and respected across the country. Changing the brand would be a step backwards.

We acknowledged that the QSPELL name was known, but we knew it was not universally respected. QSPELL was still associated with Alliance Quebec in many people's minds, and there were by this time many Anglophones as well as Francophones who took a dim view of Alliance Quebec. We had created a link to UNEQ and the Francophone literary milieu in organizing Write pour écrire. Changing the QSPELL name would help strengthen those ties.

Other points of contention were the mission of the organization and the composition of the board. Having struggled to create FEWQ as a writers' organization in 1992 and 1993, some of us wanted to be sure the new organization would be a writers' organization, with at least half the board member positions designated for professional writers. The QSPELL supporters, of whom only a few were writers, preferred the idea of a community organization with a board representing different community interests.

The fact that the CALQ funding for a writers' organization was made available almost as soon as FEWQ was incorporated led to a spike in membership. Some of the writers who have become stalwart members of the community came over to our side. FEWQ attracted support from writers who had not been enamoured of QSPELL.

A couple of important annual general meetings later, the merger was in 1998 agreed to by the boards and the membership of both QSPELL and FEWQ, and Diana McNeill, the QSPELL administrator, moved gracefully into a new role as the QWF administrator.

Suspicions took a while to die down. Encouraged by disgruntled former QSPELL board members and Writers' Union members — there was a lot of rearguard action over a period of years — *The Gazette* Books editor Bryan Demchinsky (who had succeeded Mark Abley in 1990) felt it necessary to visit the office that the Quebec Writers' Federation shared with the publishers' association in the Atwater Library to observe that there were no irregularities with the book prizes under the new regime. There were no irregularities then, and there have been no irregularities since. Demchinsky was satisfied. There were no hard feelings. The literary community came together as much as it ever could under the QWF banner, and Demchinsky himself joined the board of directors after he, too, left the position of *Gazette* Books editor.

The Quebec Writers' Federation was to have the dynamism that had eluded QSPELL; it also had the respectability that would always have eluded FEWQ. Once QWF came into existence we whisked the Awards ceremony across town to the Lion d'or, where Write pour écrire had taken place. This was a gesture in the direction of contact with Francophone writers. It was also a far cry from the Ritz. The Quebec Writers' Federation would also boost membership and establish new programmes — including a mentoring programme and writing workshops — to stimulate literary activity among aspiring Quebec writers.

The Anglo literary milieu was in ferment by this time, and important changes were taking place quickly and simultaneously. We writers were changing the circumstances in which we were living and working. This was not the kind of work that would, on its own, produce literary work of any note. We were all ruefully aware that time spent on such activity was time away from writing.

Given the way in which the literary milieu had been languishing, however, it was important work. We knew that at the time, though we didn't take ourselves too seriously and were generally irreverent. We were thumbing our noses at literary authority, united in opposition to everyone who had ignored us. So it was fun, too, and companionable.

Board meetings took place at the Atwater Library, and a bunch of us — Guy Rodgers, Ann Charney, Mary Soderstrom, Peter McFarlane, Diana O'Neill, Julie Keith, Merrily Weisbord and myself, occasionally others — would adjourn to a Chinese restaurant called Lys de Szechuan around the corner on Ste. Catherine Street. There we ordered noodles and dumplings, laughed about the latest outrages, and planned our next steps. We were creating our own literary community. The writing itself would follow, and in due course it did.

There was talk among us at the time about what it was that we needed. What were the conditions conducive to writing? What did writers need in order to thrive? And what, specifically, did Montreal's Anglophone writers need? We would have to give thought not only to what writers generally need but also to what would work here, in this uniquely challenging context. There were no models anywhere that would serve English-language writers adequately in a Francophone society in North America. We weren't even aware of any other English-language writers in a minority position, and certainly not of any in such a linguistically fraught context as Montreal. We would have to make it up as we went along.

A sense of community seemed to us one important condition, however fractious the community might be. Isolation had been the hallmark of the past, when most of the writers were themselves unaware of who else was writing. The QSPELL prizes, which would henceforth be known as the QWF prizes, were highlighting the fact that good work in English was being written in Quebec. We were all learning about writers we had never heard of before, reading work we would have been unaware of without our organizations.

We had a long wish list. We wanted reviews of books by Quebec writers to appear in *The Gazette* and in the newly created *Montreal Review of Books*, which was published by the English-language publishers' association AELAQ. We knew we needed an action plan to chip away at Toronto's indifference. We wanted more support from CBC Radio, including interviews with writers and on-air reviews. Better coverage in the book trade publication *Quill & Quire*. Recognition of the special needs of the Anglophone writing and publishing milieu.

There was more: flushed by the response to Write pour écrire, we thought increased contact with the Francophone milieu essential, as were strategies for coping with Francophones who had never

thought of putting the words "Anglo," "Quebec," and "writer" together in the same sentence.

This was not just a wish list. Bit by bit, it was turning into a list of accomplishments. More and more people now started getting involved, too, and created new books, magazines, readings series, and publishing houses, all of which added to the sense that the Anglo Montreal literary milieu was getting a new lease on life.

The idea of an international literary festival that would include us was broached around the round table over the winter of 1997–1998. It came up at Writers' Union meetings, too, with some of the same cast of characters and others, as well. Journalist and non-fiction writer Elaine Kalman Naves had been to the International Festival of Authors in Toronto and thought the time was ripe for a festival in Montreal. By the late summer, Mark Abley mentioned the idea in *The Gazette* but thought it unlikely anyone could pull it off. I listened to this talk, agreeing that it would be good to have a festival. I had never actually been to a literary festival, though, and I had a different project in mind.

For I had started going around town again, not with a tape recorder this time, but with a notebook. I was visiting all the people who could help advise me on the best way to launch *Blue Metropolis*, a Canadian magazine boldly modelled on *The New Yorker* that would feature good writing on a variety of subjects and put Montreal writers on the map. Michael Kenneally, who was still teaching at Marianopolis, gave me a valuable piece of advice based on his own experience in raising the funds for Canadian Irish Studies at Concordia University: set up a network of "Friends of Blue Metropolis" to help raise support and put me in touch with the people who could advise me on funding, structure, finances, etc.

I called up Susan Valyi, who had worked with me on *Matrix*, to design a dummy issue including articles solicited from writers who were Friends. She complained about the name — it was a long name for a magazine title — but she was the only one; everyone else loved it. I talked to everyone I knew in Montreal and in Toronto about the best ways of getting the magazine up and running.

One person I mentioned it to was a colleague of mine in the John Abbott English department, Penny Ross. She told me that

her husband Arthur could do the legal work for me when I was ready to set up an organization. And she suggested I meet Cecil Rabinovitch.

Arthur Ross had been a friend of Cecil's husband Robert Rabinovitch since the days when they were growing up in Montreal and going to summer camp in the Laurentians. Robert and Ontario-born Cecil had become one of the power couples in government, as she held senior positions in the Department of Canadian Heritage when Robert was in the Privy Council office. Now back in Montreal, Cecil had recently resigned as head of the Saidye Bronfman Centre for the Arts and might, Penny thought, be interested in getting involved in my new venture.

So I called Cecil, who was business-like on the phone, and we set up an appointment to meet the following week. I arrived at her house on foot a few minutes early on what had turned out to be a bitterly cold morning, and the church bells had just finished ringing 10 o'clock when a small car turned into the driveway and pulled up. Out stepped Cecil.

She was a trim and energetic woman with two grown children and time on her hands. We sat down in her kitchen and she made coffee. She was sceptical, even prickly, but she heard me out, and I could see her sizing me up. I was checking her out, too. She asked smart questions and surprised me with her sudden bursts of humour; there was much about her that was brisk and combative, but she was thoughtful, too. She was tempted by *Blue Metropolis*, almost against her better judgment, and by the time we had finished our coffee she had thought of a few people I should meet. And as soon as it was clear that she would help, she relaxed and so did I. We would work together for seven or eight years starting that morning.

Thanks to Cecil Rabinovitch, Ann Charney, and the many others I was discussing the magazine with, I got to meet with some of the best people in the business. In Toronto I spoke to Robert Fulford, who had been editor of *Saturday Night*, Christina McCall, star political journalist, and Peter Herrndorf, then head of TVOntario. I spoke to founders and editors of existing magazines, to a couple of influential lawyers, a marketing specialist with magazine experience, funding

agencies, advertising people, designers, fundraisers, and innumerable writers and journalists.

I did not get a lot of encouragement. Magazines are notoriously difficult, one publisher said, shaking his head. What you're looking for is an angel, another sceptic told me. Most people took me seriously and were as helpful as they could be, but I could tell they thought it was a losing proposition. I pressed on. You need deep pockets to launch a magazine, I heard time and again from people who could tell I did not have deep pockets. I got conflicting advice, too. The marketing people told me the magazine should be a business and helped me create a business plan and a charter advertisers' plan. Others advised me to set up a non-profit organization in order to be eligible for some of the government funding that was available from the Quebec and Montreal arts councils to support cultural periodicals. (The Canada Council for the Arts did not insist on non-profit status in its eligibility criteria.)

Hedging my bets, still not sure which would be the smarter move, I created Blue Metropolis Foundation as a non-profit organization in June 1997 — with a three-person board consisting of myself as president, Cecil Rabinovitch as vice-president, and Arthur Ross as secretary — and simultaneously created Blue Metropolis Inc. as a business, with myself as sole owner. I devoted the following year to the quest for start-up funds for a magazine called *Blue Metropolis*.

My efforts ended in failure. The time was not right for a new Canadian print magazine, if indeed the time is ever right for Canadian print magazines. Comparable Canadian magazines in existence at the time (*Saturday Night*, *The Next City*, etc.) failed in the next few years. When the plug was pulled last year on *Gourmet* magazine, which had a million paid subscribers, I wonder that any quality magazine survives.

I was crushed. My marriage was ending and my future uncertain. I still had my teaching job, but that no longer satisfied me. It was the darkness before the dawn.

9
The City of Words

The talk about a literary festival that would include English writers from Montreal came to a head in the summer of 1998 at about the time that I was giving up on the idea of a magazine. International writers' festivals had been proliferating across Canada, but few of us Anglos had ever been invited to participate. It wasn't only Toronto any more; Vancouver, Calgary, and Winnipeg had their own festivals, too. It was the last straw for us restless Montrealers when the Ottawa International Writers' Festival was launched in September 1998. If little Ottawa could stage an international writers' festival, then — it seemed to us — Montreal was overdue for one.

But what kind of festival should it be? It was unthinkable for a Montreal festival to be entirely (or almost entirely) in English, as was the case with English-Canadian festivals in Toronto and Vancouver. It seemed to us writers a pity for a Montreal festival to be entirely in French, as was the case with the Festival de la littérature; not only did we want to appear ourselves, but we wanted international writers of English and other languages to come to Montreal to appear at such a festival. Toronto was as little interested in our work as ever, and we figured that the solution was to go international.

The experience with Write pour écrire was inspiring here; it was possible — more than that, it was really exciting — to bring people together for events that included more than just one language. Montreal seemed the perfect city for that kind of interaction. One

thing was clear: it would be necessary to invent a new kind of literary festival for Montreal, one that would cross the linguistic divide.

I was certainly interested in a Montreal festival that would promote the work of English-language writers, and that would allow us to rub shoulders with international writers. I started considering the possibility of organizing such a festival.

As the founder of Blue Metropolis Foundation, I had a non-profit organization that could make applications for government funding. I had been one of the key people organizing Write pour écrire in two languages. I had dozens of influential Friends of Blue Metropolis, both Anglophone and Francophone, who had encouraged me in planning the magazine. I knew most of the Anglophone writers and not a few of the Francophone writers. As vice-president of the Quebec Writers' Federation, I had the practical and moral support of that organization, and I had worked with UNEQ on Write pour écrire.

What I did find daunting, when I checked on the criteria for festival funding on the Canada Council's website, was that an event had to include at least 40 writers to be considered a festival. In addition to Write pour écrire, I had by this time organized a literary series for QWF, but that was on a modest scale. The sheer logistics of organizing a festival were hard to imagine.

I didn't let that stop me. What seemed important was to start up a festival that would welcome both English-speaking and French-speaking Montrealers — and that would be open to the world. In the summer of 1998, I proposed to the board of directors of Blue Metropolis Foundation that we focus on creating a literary festival. The board approved of this new direction.

I had a conversation with Gordon Platt, the head of Writing and Publishing at the Canada Council for the Arts, and proposed a festival that would take place in French and in English in Montreal. He heard me out and made two recommendations. One was that we plan our festival for the spring, for there were already too many literary events in the fall and the writers could not manage any more. The other was that we work with UNEQ's festival.

UNEQ had made it clear that they were not interested in including us in their own festival; perhaps they would work with us again in a different context. Perhaps we could collaborate with the

Festival de la littérature for some events in two languages. Their next festival was planned for April 24-May 2, 1999.

I requested a meeting with UNEQ to discuss collaboration on this new venture, and set about preparing the first grant application in time for the Canada Council's September deadline. The name was to be the Montreal International Literary Festival / Festival littéraire international de Montréal. The dates I proposed were April 21-25, 1999. That would mean the first few days would be international, and we could collaborate with UNEQ on the weekend of April 24-25, the first days of the Festival de la littérature.

Nicole Blouin, our contact at UNEQ, had moved on by this time, so we had lost our emissary to the management and board. They took a long time getting back to us, and it was October by the time we were summoned to the Maison des écrivains to meet, for the first time ever, with the top brass.

Bruno Roy had stepped down after ten years on the job, and novelist Louis Gauthier had taken over as president. Ann Charney was now a member of the board of directors of Blue Metropolis Foundation, and she and I met with Gauthier, his vice-president, François Jobin, and the *directeur général* Pierre Lavoie in the light-filled attic boardroom. Peter McFarlane had been elected as Chair of the Writers' Union of Canada, and since Write pour écrire had officially been a collaboration between the two writers' unions, we invited him to join us.

One result was understandable confusion over who exactly we represented. Not the Writers' Union of Canada. Not the Quebec Writers' Federation, although the UNEQ people were interested in hearing about the new organization. They asked a number of questions about the English-speaking literary world we came from. They wanted to know about relations between QWF and the Writers' Union of Canada. When they understood we were there to represent Blue Metropolis Foundation, they wanted to know what Blue Metropolis Foundation was, its mission, and who the other board members were. So, too, might a delegation from Mars be received at the Pentagon.

When I mentioned that Cecil Rabinovitch was a member of the board of directors, they asked what kind of name that was. I acknowledged that Cecil was an unusual name, explained that it is

often a man's name, and then cited Cecil Rhodes as an example. It was an extraordinarily ill-chosen example, under the circumstances, given the reference René Lévesque had once famously made to Anglo-Quebecers as "white Rhodesians." Fortunately, the name Cecil Rhodes went unremarked.

Louis Gauthier wanted to know how far we had got in our planning for the festival, and they all listened closely when I reported on the partnerships I had by this time established with such organizations as the Literary Translators' Association of Canada, the Goethe Institute, and The British Council. We reminded the UNEQ brass about how well we had worked together on Write pour écrire, and they acknowledged that that had been a success. "We would like to work together again," we said, "and be able to plan some events in collaboration with the Festival de la littérature."

They were hesitant. This did not surprise us; it had taken several meetings with Blouin before the planning for Write pour écrire had started to go well. We talked some more, and they looked at one another, clearly uneasy. We were anxious to oblige, so keen were we to work with UNEQ again on this new project.

Louis Gauthier expressed doubt about the possibility of overlapping dates. Pierre Lavoie requested that we change the name of our festival, and to this we agreed. It is thanks to Pierre Lavoie that our festival came to be called the Blue Metropolis Montreal International Literary Festival / Festival littéraire international de Montréal Metropolis bleu.

We went on our way with a vague promise of meeting again, but without any commitment. We weren't overly concerned. We'd been here before. It would take time for them to come round, but they would surely come round. It was such a good idea, just as Write pour écrire had been a good idea. UNEQ had been delighted with how that worked out, and they would be delighted with how this festival collaboration would work out. I continued with the planning for the Festival, confident that we would find a way of winning UNEQ over.

I was extremely busy that fall, on unpaid leave from John Abbott College, working full-time — practically round the clock — from my home office as president and artistic director of Blue Metropolis Foundation. I sent invitations to writers, created a database, and

developed the programme of the first festival, which would eventually include a total of 57 writers. I created a festival committee of interested volunteers capable of working together in French and English, and an honorary board consisting of some of the Friends of Blue Metropolis I had enlisted on behalf of the magazine.

There was input from other Blue Metropolis Foundation board members, especially from Ann Charney and her impressive network of contacts among Francophone intellectuals, but most of the time I was working alone. The Quebec Writers' Federation helped in a couple of crucial ways, and one or two of the applications for government funding went in under the QWF name, since QWF had been incorporated under the QSPELL name for long enough to be eligible.

I made arrangements with the Europa Hotel, where the festival would take place, and met with numerous other potential partners and sponsors. The Goethe Institut had been the first to offer support, although the director, Kurt Forster, later confessed he thought I must have been mad to think I could pull off a literary festival in French and English in Montreal. The British Council offered support shortly afterwards. The Consulat de France à Québec was hesitant.

UNEQ holds its elections in November, and that fall Louis Gauthier stepped down after two years as president. The upset winner in the 1998 election was feminist poet and playwright Denise Boucher, who had become notorious 20 years earlier for her controversial play *Les fées ont soif.*

I invited Denise Boucher in person to participate in the first Blue Metropolis Montreal International Literary Festival. She perked up at that, as writers do when they get an invitation. She did not say no, and I took that as a yes, which was when things started to go wrong. I was preparing a preliminary leaflet on the festival and included Denise Boucher's name. This did not seem like a serious mistake at the time, but it was.

Many of the people I was talking to in those months leading up to the first festival were interested in the name Blue Metropolis. Why — they wanted to know — is the Metropolis *blue?*

I had read a philosophical essay called *On Being Blue* by the American writer William H. Gass when I was a student in the 1970s,

and I had been struck especially by the way in which the essay begins: two or more pages that simply list dozens of the ways that "blue" is used in English, from blue collar to blue chip, and from blue skies and blue movies to Bluenose and the blues.

What remained with me about *On Being Blue*, all those years later, was the sense that blue had countless meanings, many of them not only different in different contexts but often contradictory to one another. Where other colours — environmental green, Ukrainian orange, Communist red, etc. — have at least one clear identifier that limits their connotations, blue is wide open. Open to interpretation, as I soon discovered when I told people the name.

One Francophone writer associated "blue" with smoke: "Blue Metropolis is obviously a Montreal organization," he said; "no one smokes in Toronto." Others thought the blue in Blue Metropolis was the blue of Quebec's *fleur de lys* or the blue of the sky — *le ciel est bleu*. An American visitor thought the blue had something to do with economic hardships and boarded-up shops on Ste. Catherine Street. And a European surprised me by suggesting it was the blue of the waters around the island of Montreal; those waters had never looked blue to me.

Blue Metropolis can accommodate all these meanings and dozens of others; it is limited to none of them. Blue Metropolis, in fact, is a bit like one of the inkblots the Swiss psychologist Hermann Rorschach proposed as a test of a patient's emotional state in that it generates very different interpretations, which can be far more revealing about the person making the interpretation than they are about the inkblot itself. Blue Metropolis is a city that is open to all.

So Blue Metropolis is a utopian idea. It's the city we want to live in, or at least it's the city I want to live in. Blue Metropolis would bridge the linguistic divides of Montreal. It would bring Montrealers of different backgrounds together for literary events that would take place in French or English or both at once. It had worked with Write pour écrire; why would it not work for Blue Metropolis? I knew there was an audience for this. What I was about to learn is that not everyone would find the idea as appealing as I did.

It was an audacious project, especially since I had never actually been to a literary festival. This is one of the reasons Blue Metropolis

is not at all like other literary festivals. It could not be like any other literary festival. It emerged out of the uniqueness of Montreal, which is an ideal spot for a truly international literary festival.

Other literary festivals took place entirely, or mostly, in just one language, and there was no way that Blue Metropolis was going to take place in just one language. It would have been a pity to limit ourselves to English in a city in which Anglophones are a minority within a minority, and there was no question of us organizing a festival entirely in French. There was already a French-language festival in existence. And we wanted to be able to include Anglo writers, after all.

When Denise Boucher curtly declined to participate in the upcoming Blue Metropolis Festival, Ann Charney and I returned to the Maison des écrivains for a meeting on January 12, 1999 in the hope of resolving misunderstandings.

We then learned that the dates of UNEQ's festival had been moved to late May. The artistic director Michèle Corbeil had asked for the change because she was scheduled to programme the events for Quebec writers at the Printemps du Québec during the Salon du livre de Paris in March 1999; there was a further need to change the date, Pierre Lavoie told us, because of the availability in May of one of the Maisons de la culture where certain events would take place.

That was a disappointment. There was now no possibility of collaboration with the Festival de la littérature. It was not the end of the world, though. We could still work in partnership with UNEQ, even if the dates precluded any possibility of joint events in 1999. We could promote the Festival de la littérature, and it would be helpful to us if UNEQ were to promote our festival. This mattered to us partly because it would indeed be of practical help to us for UNEQ to send out a promotional flyer for Blue Metropolis, but even more because we wanted to work with UNEQ and to be seen as working with UNEQ. Working together, across linguistic boundaries, was a large part of the point of what we were doing.

We expressed the hope that we might work together in 2000 and said we would be happy to work under the umbrella of UNEQ. Each Festival would retain its own identity, and there could be some joint programming in French and English. In the meantime, we hoped for cross-promotion and the moral support of UNEQ.

Boucher sat at the head of the board table. She was unmoved. We explained where this idea had come from, and recounted the history of Write pour écrire and our efforts to persuade UNEQ to include in their festival those of us who could speak French. As Anglophone Quebec writers, we explained, we had long wished for a festival that would include us.

This prompted a response. "As Anglophone writers," she said, "you are not part of Quebec literature." This seemed obvious to her. This was not the first time I had heard something along such lines — her view was not far from the more nuanced view Gilles Marcotte had expressed at the Université de Montréal colloquium in 1997 — but it had never sounded quite so stark before. "You are part of English-Canadian literature, and you should look to Toronto rather than Montreal for a festival that might include you."

Where to begin to respond? Charney and I looked at each other. "But we live here in Montreal, not in Toronto. We are Montrealers."

"I don't get invited to participate in events in Toronto," Boucher persisted. "Why should you be invited in Montreal?"

"There is in fact a Salon du livre de Toronto," I pointed out. "You could be invited to read there."

"Besides," Charney said, "we are talking about participating in your festival in French, not in English. Some of us have been translated into French, and some of us speak French."

Boucher said nothing to that.

Funding was a worrying issue. We had received our $5,000 cheque from the Canada Council, but I had not spent any of it. I was not yet sure the festival would really happen, and I was afraid I might be expected to return the money if it didn't. We were still awaiting news from the various other grant applications I had made to the City of Montreal, the Conseil des arts de la Communauté urbaine de Montréal, the Conseil des arts et des lettres du Québec, and Human Resources and Development Canada.

Cecil Rabinovitch, who had made a valiant effort to raise funds for *Blue Metropolis* magazine, was discouraged at the fundraising prospects for the festival. That worried me, especially since I could by this time see the potential of the festival idea. We clearly needed help

on the fundraising front. I called up Patterson Webster, whom I knew from the board of the Quebec Writers' Federation, and we arranged to meet.

Patterson Webster was one of many who had declined to get involved in the magazine, the Websters having been burned by financial losses at *Saturday Night*. She was a southern belle from Virginia who had met Norman Webster, one-time editor of *The Globe and Mail* and of *The Gazette*, when they were students in London. She had a grown family of five, an MA in creative writing from Concordia and an avid interest in the garden of her country house in North Hatley. The festival idea grabbed her imagination at once. "You and I have to have lunch with Reford MacDougall," she declared.

I had gone to MacDougall, too, when I was looking for ways and means to get the magazine up and running. He had also been cool to that idea. A businessman from an old Montreal family, he was an enthusiast and Francophile married to a Frenchwoman.

Where the magazine had been a tough sell, the festival idea had wings. MacDougall signed on. Blue Metropolis Foundation now had a formidable private-sector fundraising team consisting of Cecil Rabinovitch, Patterson Webster, and Reford MacDougall. They would raise funds for Blue Met over the next several years on a volunteer basis, Webster focusing on foundations, MacDougall on individuals, and Rabinovitch on corporations. It is thanks to them that revenues from the private sector were from that first year onward approximately equal to revenues from government agencies.

By the time Webster and I had lunch with MacDougall, I was so run off my feet that I could hardly find time to think about hiring anyone to help me in the preparations for the festival. I was feeling more confident now that we would get more money. In mid-February 1999 the writer Julie Keith — who was a member of the Festival committee — and I interviewed three candidates.

One of these candidates was Peter McFarlane, who agreed to work on a contract basis at $10 per hour. One person clearly wasn't going to be enough, and one week later I signed another contract, this time for an assistant, Chantal Bourbon. It was full-tilt for all three of us from that point on until opening night on April 21. The programme was finalized by the beginning of February, and I hired a

publicist to get the word out. We were in the home stretch, and the last thing we needed was a crisis, but that is what we got.

A document I had prepared when I thought Denise Boucher had agreed to participate in the festival — and then withdrawn when she wrote to decline the invitation — came into the hands of UNEQ.

First, I had a call from Denise Boucher and then received an ice-cold letter signed by *directeur général* Pierre Lavoie severing relations between UNEQ and Blue Metropolis.[33] I spoke to nationalist writer and UNEQ member Yves Beauchemin, who was one of the writers who had agreed to participate in the festival. They had all conferred with one another and other UNEQ members, and the upshot was clear. The Blue Metropolis Festival was seen as a federalist plot — *un complot fédéraliste* — designed to undermine the French language and culture of Quebec. I was "the Stéphane Dion of the literary milieu" — a reference to the federal Minister of Intergovernmental Affairs who became the bane of the nationalists in the wake of the 1995 Referendum.[34]

All this was entirely unexpected and alarming, in the weeks leading up to our first festival, and it created considerable anxiety about our government funding, about the festival's reputation as a literary event, and — most crucially of all — about the success of the festival as an event bringing Francophones and Anglophones together. I had thought of Blue Metropolis as a bigger and better version of Write pour écrire. I saw myself as responding to post-referendum calls for Anglos to play a more active role in Quebec. I was all set to promote the French language and literature of Quebec on an international stage. The very last thing I had expected was to be seen as plotting to undermine the French language and culture of Quebec.

Some 29 Francophones, almost all of them members of UNEQ, had confirmed their participation in the festival by March 3. UNEQ now circulated recent correspondence between UNEQ and Blue Metropolis to its members with a cover letter I have not seen. What followed was a terrible week when it was not clear how many festival participants were going to cancel. Yves Beauchemin faxed me a letter on March 4 to say that he was cancelling because of the lack of transparency shown by the use of the UNEQ name in festival publicity.[35]

The playwright and author Jean-Claude Germain, who has irreproachably nationalist credentials, used his reputation to defend us. France Théoret picked up the phone to call me and find out what had happened. She told me what she had learned about the issues, and from whom, and clearly disapproved of the tactics used to discredit Blue Metropolis. She offered her support and confirmed that she would honour her commitment to participate in the festival.

Four writers cancelled. Though the timing suggests that all four did so as a result of the problem with UNEQ, only two of them — Yves Beauchemin and Hélène Pelletier-Baillargeon — actually referred to UNEQ in their cancellations. I was able to replace four writers without difficulty.

In addition to worrying about UNEQ and its members, I had to consider the reaction of my volunteers to these developments. They were anxious, and I understood why. The basis of their interest — most people's interest — in Blue Metropolis was that we would be successful in crossing the linguistic divide. I kept the board and other volunteers informed, with the result that we ended up both more unified and more determined than ever.

It was now mid-March. External communications had to kick in if we were going to get the public to attend our festival. The publicist hired just the previous week now resigned, however, as a direct result of the conflict with UNEQ. She was a Francophone who had done work for UNEQ, and she was afraid she would be blacklisted if she were to work for us. Ann Charney had heard of a publicist who had worked for the Canadian Centre for Architecture, and we promptly engaged the services of Communications Dion & LeBlanc. Marie-José LeBlanc had five weeks to publicize the first Blue Metropolis Montreal International Literary Festival.

In the midst of the crisis, I set off for the Salon du livre de Paris for a few days, where Quebec was guest of honour and the Printemps du Quebec had begun. There I was able to hobnob with many of the writers who would be part of Blue Met and attract the interest of literary journalist Jean Fugère, whom I had seen in the lobby of the Maison des écrivains on my first visit there before Write pour écrire. I invited him to host a festival event, and he readily agreed. I talked to many others, and the notoriety of Blue Metropolis in literary circles

by this time was such that I could tell as soon as I introduced myself who was open to Blue Metropolis and who was not.

My presence in Paris did surprise a couple of UNEQ stalwarts, including Pierre Lavoie, the *directeur général* of UNEQ, who was manning the Quebec stand when I made my first tour of the Salon du livre. We had had no contact since his letter at the beginning of the débâcle three weeks earlier. When I spotted Yves Beauchemin ahead of me in one of the long aisles, I called out, "*Monsieur Yves Beauchemin!*" in a friendly voice that attracted the attention of a few Parisian book lovers and publishers at nearby stands, and I chatted with him for a few minutes. I was happy to be in Paris and happy in the knowledge that the festival was going ahead.

By this time, funding for the first Blue Metropolis Festival from both the Conseil des arts de la Communauté urbaine de Montréal and the Conseil des arts et des lettres du Québec had been confirmed. We had already received a grant from the Canada Council and would shortly receive one from the National Literacy Secretariat at Human Resources Development Canada for our literacy and community writing activities. So we did indeed receive funding from all levels of government, though not from the Department of Canadian Heritage, for we were not eligible. I mention this because of persistent and unfounded allegations that we had political and financial support from Sheila Copps, then Minister of Canadian Heritage.

The persistence of the view of Blue Metropolis as a federalist plot is ironic, given that UNEQ and its festival had received far greater amounts of federal funding than the Blue Metropolis Festival.

It is a view that does not stand up to scrutiny. Our financial books are not only audited but are inspected by many who would have been pleased to publicize any irregularity. Besides, Sheila Copps would surely have been better advised to choose a Québécoise Line Tremblay, say, rather than a woman with an obviously Anglophone name like Linda Leith, if she had really been determined to use a literary festival as a fifth column in the fight for the hearts and minds of Quebecers.

And the show did go on. The first Blue Metropolis Montreal International Literary Festival took place, as planned, April 21-25, 1999 at the Europa Hotel on Drummond Street. On opening night,

we had invited an official from the Consulat de France à Québec to speak, but he cancelled. The Consulat had been a reluctant partner from the start, and the official had been hard to reach ever since the souring of relations with UNEQ.

There were events with the great American novelist Russell Banks, who appeared for the same token sum everyone else was offered, and with Jovette Marchessault, one of the legendary figures of Quebec literature I had read and written about, in conversation with the radio and television host Christiane Charette. Writers Myrna Kostash, Maggie Siggins, and Jean-Claude Germain all participated, along with Indian writer Amitav Ghosh, three writers from Northern Ireland, and a number of Anglo Quebec writers with recent books, including Julie Keith, Ann Charney, Peter McFarlane, Mary Soderstrom, and David Homel. Among the audience members was Stanley Péan, who would become president of UNEQ in 2004. The first festival included 57 writers participating in events in English or French, with some events — including what would become our signature Blue Metropolis Translation Slam — taking place in both languages.

We had better press in English than in French, and a bigger turnout for events in English. In part this was because there were so few other events that included English-language writers, whereas there had always been lots of literary activity in French, so there was far greater competition both at the outset in 1999 and later on for Francophone audiences. Blue Metropolis was and is a much bigger deal for English-speaking Montrealers than for Francophones, partly because it is known to be an Anglophone initiative, and partly because there are so many more other events in French for Francophones to choose from.

The novelty of a festival that included both languages — we never called it a "bilingual festival," though that is what it was in that first year — was also more appealing to English Quebecers than to Francophones, who are far more likely to regard "bilingualism" askance. Politics played a role, as well, in this as in so much else, and we came to be regarded as "the federalist festival" in contrast to the Festival de la littérature, which was "the nationalist festival." It was misleading to call us "federalist" when so many of the festival participants had solid "indépendantiste" credentials. What was most telling was that we were being firmly associated with one side, where what we had wanted was to bridge divides as we had done with Write pour écrire in 1996.

Over the five days, we attracted a respectable total of 1,500 people. On the Sunday afternoon, as the last event was winding down and people were filing out of the hotel, the Canada Council officer Carole Boucher told me, "You have a festival," which I took to mean that Blue Metropolis would be accepted for festival funding, as indeed it has been ever since.

We had put together a total of $112,000, of which about half came from government sources and the rest from the private sector, with some revenues from ticket sales. I had not been paid for my work — I had not asked to be paid, not knowing what revenues we would have until after the dust settled. When we ended up with a modest budgetary surplus, the board of directors voted after the Festival to pay me the sum of $10,000 for the work I had done over the previous year; that left us with enough to start the planning for 2000. I would be paid increasing amounts from this point on, as revenues increased.

I had had many leaves of absence from John Abbott College over the years, and in 2000 the boom came down, and I was compelled to choose between full-time teaching at John Abbott and quitting altogether. It was impossible to teach full-time and also do the work required to build Blue Metropolis. I agonized over this and went out to Ste-Anne-de-Bellevue in a vain attempt to enlist the support of the college and the union for my work with Blue Metropolis. I had by this point earned a total of $20,000 in the previous 18 months of work for Blue Metropolis, and the future of Blue Metropolis was far from secure.

Eventually, with a heavy heart, I quit my teaching position. It would be three more years before I was earning as much from Blue Metropolis as I had earned as a member of the English department of John Abbott College. I signed my first employment contract with Blue Metropolis Foundation in March 2004, a few weeks before the opening of the 6th annual Blue Metropolis Montreal International Literary Festival.

10
The Nationalist Response

The UNEQ crisis had a lasting impact on Blue Metropolis, for good and for ill, and uneasy relations persisted for several years.

I had been at fault in the matter of Denise Boucher, certainly. I had understood her to say she agreed to participate in the festival; I should not have mentioned her name in any documentation until I had written confirmation. That I did so was a question of bad judgment and inexperience. I had simply not realized how much that mattered. The problem with UNEQ had deeper roots, however. There has, after all, been no other such mistake on our part, and there were later difficulties.

There were no reports in the press at the time of the crisis; some did appear later, either amused or incredulous or, in one rare instance, thoughtful. That was an article written by Alberto Manguel a year afterwards.

Comical as this war seemed to some observers, this was a serious battle, as both UNEQ and we at Blue Metropolis were aware at the time. One way of looking at it is as a battle over the definition of Quebec literature. UNEQ was defending the view that Quebec literature was French, by definition. We were countering with a new definition: that Quebec literature was French and that it was — or it should be — also open to English and other languages. I think it's fair to say that there was a lot more at stake, as well, and that literature

was a flashpoint for the much broader question of what it means to be a Quebecer.

Alberto Manguel participated in the second Blue Metropolis Festival in April 2000 and published an article the following week in *The Globe and Mail*. The article begins with an account of the exuberance of the festival itself and its extraordinary mix of languages.

> All this versatility, richness, variety and scope of multilingualism was constantly in evidence throughout the Blue Metropolis Festival. Not everyone, however, shared this jubilant view.

Manguel goes on to mention the past collaboration with UNEQ on Write pour écrire. But this year, Boucher evidently "decided things would be different." UNEQ wished, Manguel reported, not to work under what she saw as "an Anglo umbrella."

Boucher's allegation that we had wanted UNEQ to work under an Anglo umbrella was not only false; it was also sure to damn us in the eyes of self-respecting Francophones.

The truth is that Blue Metropolis had no "umbrella" at the time. Blue Metropolis was not a viable organization in the lead-up to the first festival. It was nothing more than a hope and a prayer. It had made financial commitments for the planned festival in the months prior to the festival that far exceeded actual resources; it had no paid staff, no office, no track record, and no reputation. Blue Metropolis was an entirely quixotic project, and few would have given it much hope of survival. It would have been unthinkable for Blue Metropolis to ask UNEQ to work under the umbrella of what was at the time an Anglophone organization. As before, in the case of Write pour écrire, we were the supplicants. We were anxious to oblige and to collaborate with UNEQ under almost any conditions they cared to name.

Most Québécois trust the importance of their culture, Manguel argues, and consider it deserves an international stage, "one which festivals like Blue Metropolis are eager to offer it." He cites as evidence our 2000 festival tribute to Anne Hébert and the awarding of our inaugural Blue Metropolis International Literary Grand Prix to Marie-Claire Blais. Boucher's faith in her own culture, he suggests, is alarmingly slim, since she fears it might simply vanish when confronted with other cultures. While cultures do have to beware of aggression, there is "a vast

difference between aggression and dialogue," and "the organizers of Blue Metropolis merely proposed the latter." Manguel concludes his article with a cautionary episode from 8th century Chinese history, when two armies, one from the north and one from the south, agree on a short truce and set up camp not far from each other:

> Suddenly, the soldiers of the southern faction heard the soldiers of the northern faction gathered around the campfire, singing the southerners' songs, and at once the southern faction realized that they had lost the war.

Those of us at Blue Metropolis have been called many things, but never before or since have we been called soldiers of the northern faction. The analogy is apt, though; as Anglophones working in French, we were indeed singing the southerners' songs.

The Blue Metropolis Montreal International Literary Festival remains to this day unique in the world in its use of language; such other multilingual festivals as have come into existence translate the writers' words, whereas we bring in the public that speaks those languages so that the festival public itself is multilingual. Such a festival could probably never have emerged elsewhere than in Montreal. While its origins are clearly Anglophone, and it is right to acknowledge that it is an English Montreal initiative, it has always sought to bridge the linguistic divide and reflect the linguistic complexity of Montreal. Programming has from the start been more French than English, and there have always been more Francophone than Anglophone participants. Both the festival itself and extra-festival programming have often had a larger Francophone than Anglophone public, and the Children's Festival, which came into being in 2007, is more than 80 per cent French.

It's a complicated identity in a complicated city. From the point of view of Blue Metropolis, what matters is to do what we can to ensure that the perception is accurate. Blue Metropolis is, however, still widely perceived by Quebec Francophones and Anglophones alike as an Anglophone organization. While there are understandable reasons for this, it is inaccurate to consider Blue Metropolis as simply an Anglophone organization, and we have gone out of our way to change the perception.

The reasons people see Blue Metropolis as an Anglophone organization are clear. One is that I am an Anglophone, and I have been the visible face of Blue Metropolis from the start. In fact, I was the only Anglophone on staff for several years, and am currently one of two English-speaking staff members out of a total of ten.

The board, which was mostly English-speaking at the outset, has been half French or more than half French for the past six years. That said, it has to be added that Blue Metropolis remains far more Anglophone than most other Quebec literary and cultural organizations, which are as a rule led and staffed by Francophones.

Another reason that Blue Metropolis is perceived as Anglophone is the name of the organization. Blue Metropolis was originally planned as the name of an English-language magazine and it has always been more readily accepted in English than in French. Louis Gauthier, who was president of UNEQ when we first brought the idea for a literary festival to the Maison des écrivains, commented to me in 1998 that the name might be a problem for Francophones. It's a name that prompts questions in both languages — what does it mean? why blue? etc. — but Francophones have difficulty with the name and change it to "Métropolis" when we view "Metropolis" as the title of a notable German film that takes no accent.

Then of course there is the fact that the origins of Blue Metropolis are indeed Anglophone. Good reasons, in other words. It's not only understandable but in some sense true that Blue Metropolis be perceived as Anglophone. It just isn't the whole truth.

It isn't the whole truth not only because the work of Blue Metropolis is more French than English, and not only because the writers we showcase are more French than English, but because the whole point is to break out of linguistic divides and build bridges.

Knowing the perception that Blue Metropolis is Anglophone and the more complicated truth of what Blue Metropolis is all about, we have made many efforts over the years to change the perception.

We have created a remarkable French-language festival programme; this has been the work of my dear colleague Ève Pariseau for the past eight years. We have staffed the office with Francophones from different backgrounds, starting with our dynamic general manager Michelle Sylvestre and including Elisabeth Reyt, Alejandro Rosales,

Florence Allegrini, Catherine St. Jacques, Annabelle Moreau, Alice van der Klei, Julie Groleau, and Isabelle Chartrand Delorme; in 2009 we added one English-speaking staff member, Sarah Tobias, as director of development. We have added French-speaking Montrealers to the board of directors and to our various committees. We have submitted our grant applications in French, even when I wrote them and it would have been less work to submit them in English. We have placed great emphasis on the quality of written French in all our communications.

We have done all this in order to gain wider acceptance in the Francophone milieu, and in some part we have succeeded. We have done what we have to counter the perception that we are simply an Anglophone organization in the same spirit in which a few of us crossed the city in 1996 and then again in 1998 and 1999 in the hope of working with UNEQ. We have done all this because we wanted to bridge the linguistic divide. Our aim is not to serve any one linguistic community; it is dedicated to serving English, French, and other linguistic communities. Most of this is well known, well understood, and widely accepted, and the work of Blue Metropolis is treated with respect and enthusiasm in most quarters.

The perception of Blue Metropolis as simply an Anglophone organization sometimes translates into an unreasonable insistence that Blue Metropolis is an organization that serves Anglophones primarily. This marginalizes Blue Metropolis and has had a negative impact on funding from Conseil des Arts et des Lettres du Québec.

The only people who have ever been unconvinced that Blue Metropolis is Anglophone, curiously, have been federal officials in charge of handing out moneys to support the official-language minority of Quebec. This funding, which was known as IPOLC funding, was based on the argument that official-language minority groups need additional support. Given the history of Blue Metropolis, it is ironic that we were for some years denied this funding until I paid a visit to Ottawa to remind the Canada Council for the Arts of our Anglophone credentials.

We have the rare distinction, in other words, of having been too English to satisfy CALQ juries and too French to satisfy federal bureaucrats meting out funding for the English-speaking minority of Quebec. This is what happens when you set out to build bridges.

Blue Metropolis has had little impact to date in English Canada, partly because we have had few resources to devote to national communications and outreach. Besides, the linguistic adventurousness that characterizes Blue Metropolis doesn't have a lot to do with the prevailing view of Canadian Literature as English-only.

The response to Blue Metropolis from Toronto has differed in some ways from that in other parts of Canada. Writers from other parts of Canada often love Blue Metropolis, I suspect because they recognize that the Festival challenges the prevailing CanLit régime based in Toronto.

The reaction from Toronto has sometimes been uncomprehending. Toronto writers who have participated in Blue Metropolis events have at times seemed mystified. It is an annual struggle to get the Toronto publishing houses with international stars to send one or two of them to Montreal for the festival. There has been some favourable attention from individual publishers, including Patrick Crean of Thomas Allen, Scott Griffin of House of Anansi, and Douglas Gibson of McClelland & Stewart, as well as writers such as Margaret Atwood, George Elliott Clarke, John Ralston Saul, and Priscila Uppal, but Blue Metropolis remains little known in English Canada and largely ignored by its media.

The most important exception is CBC Radio, which uses the largest room in the Festival hotel as a broadcast studio shared with Radio-Canada. Hosts of such national shows as "Writers & Company," "Ideas," "Sunday Morning," and "Q" come to Montreal for on-stage conversations and panel discussions with festival writers that are recorded on site and broadcast nationally thereafter. Most Canadians outside of Montreal who know of Blue Met do so because they have heard these broadcasts.

Montreal's English-language literary milieu had lived through important changes in the 1990s that had no equivalent in the Francophone milieu or in any other part of Canada. After the glory days of the 1940s and 1950s, when English writers in Quebec were the most influential in Canada and, in some cases, recognized internationally, the literary milieu suffered badly from the social and economic effects both of Canadian nationalism — which saw Toronto emerge as the rapidly growing centre of English-Canadian publishing — and of

Quebec nationalism, which contributed to the decline of Montreal. In the 1980s and well into the 1990s, the Anglophone writing and publishing world was thoroughly demoralized. It was of so little interest either to English Canada or to French Quebec in these years that it had only its own meagre resources to draw on. And draw on those it did in the struggle to pull itself up by its own bootstraps.

The Francophone milieu had not been through any equivalent changes in that period, and it was not ready for Metropolis bleu. Its own adjustment to the cultural realities of the new Quebec — with its reduced English-speaking minority and its increasingly numerous and vocal cultural communities — was only beginning in the late 1990s.

Few Francophones had — or indeed have — any real understanding of the recent history of the English-speaking milieu, its demoralization, or its internal struggles. Few would have given Montreal's English writers or writing a second thought if it had not been for the outrage provoked by Mordecai Richler in *Oh Canada! Oh Quebec!* Most Francophones had little experience of sympathizing with their English-speaking neighbours; Anglos were the historic Other and were — in some cases still are — regarded as disproportionately privileged. It may have been inevitable that there would be some suspicion of the ebullient new venture called Blue Metropolis.

The UNEQ chill continued throughout Denise Boucher's presidency, which came to an end in December 2000. We had some friends, certainly — poet Émile Martel had offered to help at the end of the first festival and did his best to intervene with UNEQ — but I was treated as a pariah in some Francophone literary circles, with people I knew crossing the room in order to avoid being seen in my company. It was deeply unpleasant. By the time poet and editor Bernard Pozier declined an invitation to participate in an event about writing about hockey planned for the second festival in 2000, I had sufficient experience of rejection and ostracism to ask him why he did not wish to participate in Blue Metropolis. He was taken aback, clearly not expecting to be queried on his decision, and the answer he then gave me was not only short and instructive but clear: "*Parce que vous êtes anglophone.*"

The intervening years have seen ups and downs in relations between Blue Metropolis and UNEQ. Bruno Roy was re-elected

president of UNEQ in December 2000, met with me, and made an effort to understand the problem. Friends of Blue Metropolis such as writer Jean-Claude Germain and the XYZ Éditeur publisher André Vanasse — my own publisher and the publisher of Bruno Roy among many other Quebec writers — were responsible for some successful efforts at *rapprochement*, including cross-promotion of the two festivals. Their credibility in the nationalist literary milieu and their willingness to champion a literary festival that crossed the linguistic divide helped defuse some nationalist suspicions.

There were other signs of openness. After Festival 2000 and again in 2007, Blue Metropolis was the literary nominee for the Grand Prix du livre de Montréal. I was invited to participate in the Rencontre québécoise internationale des écrivains and to contribute to the literary magazine *Arcade*; both the quality and the quantity of media coverage in French increased with each festival; and other respected Francophones, notably Leméac publisher Lise Bergevin and Simone Sauren, then publicity manager of Groupe Ville-Marie, as well as several distinguished writers such as Louise Dupré, Naïm Kattan, and Lise Gauvin had the courage — it did take courage — to allow their names to be publicized as members of our committees even in the early days. Other distinguished Francophones, including Mireille Goulet, Johanne Pérusse, Maurice Forget, Vivianne de Kinder, Pierre-André Themens, Isabelle Fontaine, and Suzanne Rancourt, have sat on the board of directors of Blue Metropolis Foundation.

Concerned that the proximity of the two festivals might be having a negative impact on their attendance, UNEQ tried to persuade Blue Metropolis to move its annual festival dates to the fall, and the two organizations met to discuss this and other matters of mutual interest. After due deliberation, we decided not to change our dates to the fall, which was already crowded with English-Canadian literary festivals in September and October and the Salon du livre de Montréal in November. Eventually, when what was by now called the Festival international de la littérature (FIL) was incorporated as an organization independent of UNEQ, its board decided on a September date, starting in 2005.

With all the goodwill in the world, though — and there was goodwill, on both sides — the opportunity for true collaboration between Blue Metropolis and UNEQ had been missed. In 1999

Blue Metropolis was genuinely willing to work as the poor relation to UNEQ that it then was, but it took on a life of its own after that. The two festivals had different missions and for the most part quite different audiences. We each went about our business.

Blue Metropolis was gradually becoming accepted and established in French in Quebec, as it already was in English. It was becoming accepted in some of Montreal's other linguistic communities, as well, and it was gaining an international reputation for its programming in different languages. It had become the world's first multilingual literary festival.

The hatchet was dug up and dusted off in a misbegotten political tract published in the fall of 2005. In *Le Référendum volé*, Robin Philpot, who had been communications director of the nationalist Société St-Jean-Baptiste, cites Denise Boucher and Pierre Lavoie among others in an attempt to identify Blue Metropolis with federalist strategies and political funding. It was a shock to realize the extent to which old grievances had been festering in some quarters ever since 1999, gaining in rancour if not in credibility.

The UNEQ newsletter that appeared at the end of the year contributed further to the politicization of Blue Metropolis. "*Drôle d'alliance*," signed by the board of directors of UNEQ, refers to Blue Metropolis as doing a good job of serving the federal government's bilingualism and biculturalism objectives";[36] a column signed by Bernard Pozier in the same issue adds a nationalist twist to the multiple meanings of "blue" in Blue Metropolis: in referring to the "*mal coloré Blue Metropolis (plutôt Red ?)*," he associates Blue Metropolis with Liberal red. Echoes here of Maurice Duplessis saying, "*Le ciel est bleu, l'enfer est rouge*" — even if the "bleu" was now the blue of the Parti Québécois rather than the Union nationale.

Most commentators have argued that UNEQ's opposition to Blue Metropolis is a question of economics. David Homel argues in *La Presse* in 2003 that the war was all about money, about the struggle for funding: "Funds are the sinews of war. What we're witnessing is a battle over government grants. If Blue Metropolis applies for a certain amount from a government agency and UNEQ asks the same, who will come out on top?"[37] A similar argument appears in *Le Devoir* in March 2006, where Norman Thériault speaks of financing for two

literary festivals in a city where there was supposed to be one festival for each discipline.[38]

There are political reasons as well. These have to do with the perceived federalism of Blue Metropolis, as comments reported by Philpot and expressed by Pozier make explicit. Blue Metropolis was created by Anglophones. We have always been clear about that and proud of it. It's also undeniably true that most Anglophones are federalists, and it has evidently been important for some of those around UNEQ to politicize Blue Metropolis. Broader political reasons have to do with what constitutes Quebec writing and with attitudes towards Anglophones and their place in Quebec literature and Quebec society.

Blue Metropolis would surely have been more readily accepted if it had taken place only in English, especially if it had been content to remain small and unassuming. Blue Metropolis would likely have been more readily accepted if it had indeed been a federalist plot, so long as it remained on the English side of town. Our sin — and the reason that a handful of nationalists have taken such an interest in us — was that we did successfully cross linguistic divides. Our sin was in moving into the Quartier latin in 2000, when we headed east from the Europa Hotel on Drummond to the Hôtel des Gouverneurs on St. Hubert. Our sin was in being big and bold and international and multilingual. And still, in part, Anglophone.

There are worse sins. In a very few if memorable cases, there has been suspicion. Far more common is warmth and enthusiasm. And once in a while I am aware of something less easily defined. I occasionally have the impression that the Quebecer I am talking to is not really sure what to do with me or with Blue Metropolis.

Blue Metropolis is popular with all but a small circle of people. There were officers in Quebec government agencies who went out of their way to congratulate us when we moved into the Quartier latin. There are countless festival-goers, Francophone and non-Francophone, who are happy with what Blue Metropolis represents. Some Francophones wept to see events with authors — Paul Auster, for example — they adored. What makes Blue Metropolis unpopular with some of the nationalists is not, I think, any supposed allegiance to a single point of view, political or otherwise. What makes Blue

Metropolis unpopular in those small circles is, I would suggest, its openness to many points of view, its quality, its appeal, and the fact that it does a better job than most of putting Quebec writers on an international stage.

If Blue Metropolis provoked a hostile reaction in some quarters, it has been welcomed by many Montrealers with open arms. It is today attracting more, and more favourable, commentary in the French-language media than ever before. It draws 14,000-17,000 people in any given year and has set attendance records for a multi-genre literary festival in Canada. For all the suspicion of Blue Metropolis and all the hostility it has inspired, it has also generated sympathy and interest and growing affection. Openness and diversity, conviviality and ebullience are attractive qualities, after all. And they are qualities that Montrealers pride themselves on. Montrealers have reason to be proud of Blue Metropolis.

The unshakeable Anglophone identity may perhaps have played its own part here, as well. The fact that Blue Metropolis has always been identified as Anglophone has not always, or not only, hurt Blue Metropolis. It might be that it matters little who it is who created a festival, who organizes it, and what language they speak at home, so long as the festival is good. That in itself would be encouraging, if unlikely in a society as politicized as this one. It might even be that there is greater appreciation of Blue Metropolis in some quarters *because* it is in part Anglophone and because it is seen as an Anglophone organization that has extended its hand across the city. Though we suffered some anxiety over Philpot's attack in 2005, we soon came to see that we had nothing to fear. The attacks backfired. If they succeeded in anything, it was in generating sympathy for Blue Metropolis and in undermining the credibility of the attackers.

There might, in other words, be a growing sense of appreciation of — and even sympathy for — Anglophones, their role, and their place in the new Quebec. I would like to think it is so. And if it is so, this is something that has been changing. And to the extent that this has been changing, the change has come about in some part because of Blue Metropolis itself. Blue Metropolis has succeeded in making the writers and the diverse people of Quebec known to one another in a way that was previously unimaginable. Anglophone readers know and appreciate their Francophone neighbours that bit better because

of Blue Metropolis; Francophone readers know and appreciate their Anglophone neighbours that bit better, too. Blue Metropolis has opened both of these communities to each other and to many others. Blue Metropolis is a case study in the acceptance of Anglophones by the Francophone majority, prompting the greater appreciation of those of us who live and write in English in Quebec.

The appropriate role for an English-speaking writer in 1999 was evidently not to suggest working with UNEQ on an international festival that would include English. Not so far as UNEQ itself was concerned, anyway. The appropriate role for an English-speaking writer was evidently not to head up a festival that would become internationally recognized for its programming in French, English, and other languages.

And yet no one but an English-speaking writer would have done it. No one but an English-speaking writer would have had any interest in promoting writing in English. No one but an English-speaking writer would have belonged to a literary community with a sufficiently substantial history in Montreal to dare to propose an international literary festival that would take place not only in French but also in English and other languages. No one but an English-speaking writer — a member of the demoralized English-language literary world — would have had the need, in the late 1990s, to put heart and soul into such a utopian project as Blue Metropolis and make it work.

11
Revival

In the golden age of the 1940s and 1950s, there were English Montreal writers who had to make it in New York or in London before their talent could be recognized at home in Canada. Quebec's *Grande noirceur* ended with the death of Maurice Duplessis in 1959 and the new broom of Jean Lesage's Liberal government swept away the Catholic Church and some of the English business interests that had been profiting under the old regime.

Many English-speaking Quebecers applauded as Quebec seized the reins of its own future, but terrorist bombs in Westmount in the early 1960s and the 1970 FLQ kidnappings of cabinet minister Pierre Laporte and British consul general James Cross created a sense of foreboding. The sovereignist Parti Québécois elected its first government in November 1976, and the passing of the Charter of the French Language in 1977 was likely the nadir for Anglos, the darkest days of its own *Noirceur minoritaire*, when Anglos faced the reality of their own diminished status as an English-speaking minority within Quebec. For writers, the light at the end of this tunnel would only start to glimmer at the close of the millennium.

The work on English-language fiction that I undertook in the 1980s focused on the writers themselves and their published work. I published essays, articles on some individual writers, and on what I had come to see as the extraordinary situation that Anglo writers were in at the time. It was too soon to write a book on the subject, in

part because the story was still evolving, and in part because it was too soon for me to undertake a book of such range.

Of such range? A book focusing on Montreal's English-language fiction might not seem to be a book of any great range. When I began my work, it seemed highly specialized, even obscure, and in some ways it is. Canadian literature is already a fairly narrow specialty in the scheme of things, even if we include writing in French as well as in English. The fact that it is rare for Canadian literature to have this inclusive meaning has contributed to the problem we in Montreal have had to deal with — and to the problem that Canada faces.

Within the field of Canadian literature, English Montreal fiction must seem narrower still, except that this is not only a literary story. It's a story about the effect of two rival nationalisms. And it's a story of how a community found itself underground when its language became invisible and the work of its writers was reduced to the status of a very minor literature indeed. The fact that the language in question is English, the most powerful language on earth, adds curiosity, incongruity, and comedy to the invisibility of Montreal's English writers. For anyone interested in the mysterious links between literature and social change, however, this is a remarkable case study. And the fact that one of the most spectacular successes emerging out of English Montreal in recent years has turned out to be a literary festival is only one irony among many. What it means is that an effective field of endeavour for English-speaking Montrealers was one in which we were of little importance to anyone inside or outside of Quebec. The very insignificance of what we English-language writers were doing turned out to be one of the secrets of our success.

People love to cheer for the underdog, and in some ways we were the underdog. As William Weintraub found out when he published a dystopian novel about English-speaking Montreal called *The Underdogs* in 1985, not everyone cheered. Francophone nationalists in particular were not amused (Leith 1986). To the nationalists, English-speaking Montrealers like Weintraub were the top dogs. They themselves — the Francophones — were the underdogs. Victim status could hardly be more sought after if it had been the Nobel Prize.

There is truth to both views. English-speaking Montrealers are in some ways the underdogs and in some ways we are not the

underdogs. We are certainly not the only underdogs, and there are Francophones who fervently deny us the status of underdogs. We are certainly not only the underdog, either, for the English-speaking community is varied and it includes captains of industry to this day along with the disadvantaged. Our language is unpopular in some quarters, inflammatory, and either minimized or banned. A recent immigrant is more likely to get hired in some offices, including offices of government, than an Anglo whose family has lived here for generations. Whatever our family history, whatever our income, and regardless of how long we have lived here, today's English-speaking Montrealers are the victims of a historical identification between Anglos in general and that small minority who were overlords and oppressors of the majority of French-speaking Quebecers — and the majority of English-speaking Quebecers — before most of us were born.

The aim of Bill 101 was to put Francophones in charge, and it has succeeded in many ways. This is a contested topic, with much concern over a recent decrease in the number of Francophones on the island of Montreal, as young Francophones have been leaving the city for cheaper housing in off-island suburbs at the same time as young Anglophones are leaving the regions of Quebec and moving to Montreal to study and find work. A Quebec government commission mandated to assess the position of French in Quebec in the mid-1990s reached the following conclusion:

> The sociolinguistic situation of Francophone workers in the early 1970s was largely corrected by the adoption of Bill 101 in 1997, a language law viewed by its authors as a measure to restore "social justice," though other factors in Quebec also contributed to this correction. [39]

Anglophones who left as part of the great exodus voted with their feet, but most Anglophones who live here today have accepted the law and its application as we go about our daily business. English-language writers are no exception to this, except that our very business is conducted in the underground language.

Dissidence is always a good subject, and that's especially the case when set in Montreal, which has never quite lost its reputation for sin. Montreal is an enigma wrapped in a conundrum in one

corner — maybe the cornerstone, even today — of the Canadian maze. Until further notice, any notes from the Anglo underground in Montreal cannot help but comment on what we mean by Canada.

Certain aspects of the situation of Quebec Anglos are unique, among them the notable fact that here English is a minority language, the use of which in public places has been limited in law for more than three decades. This has been important in reassuring the Francophone majority that their own language will be safeguarded. It has also been responsible for creating the Montreal we know today, with all its riches, complexities, tensions, and pleasures.

Quebec Anglos also have something in common with other groups who are in a minority position — Japanese in Brazil, Blacks in the United States, and Francophones across Canada, to mention only these — and perhaps even more with other groups who form a minority within such minorities: gay Japanese in Brazil, say, or Jewish Blacks in the United States.

It was the Jews of Babylon surrounded by Arabs under the Persian Empire who produced the Talmud. It was a Jewish writer who was a member of the German-speaking minority of Prague who wrote *The Castle* and *The Trial*. Distant as these are from contemporary Montreal, they are the literary products of a minority within a minority. A closer comparison can be made with the Anglo-Irish Literary Revival that emerged out of the clash of Irish and British nationalisms over a century ago.[40]

Disadvantaged as these minority contexts clearly were in their different ways, they were also contexts with a potential that can only astonish anyone focused on the disadvantages. Who could have predicted the Babylonian Talmud or the accomplishment of Franz Kafka? Who could have predicted the Anglo-Irish Literary Revival and a Nobel Prize for the Anglo-Irish Protestant W. B. Yeats?

There is no way of knowing if today's English-speaking Quebec will produce a figure of such stature. International attention for Montreal writers does not always translate into recognition that the writers in question are in fact associated with Montreal, as noted in a recent letter to *The New York Times* by Quebec Writers' Federation executive director Lori Schubert. The fact that her letter was published, however, may contribute to increased awareness among readers of that newspaper of Montreal as home to English-language

writers as well as Francophone writers. Its greater impact might be in Montreal itself, where both *The Gazette* and the *Montreal Review of Books* reprinted the letter.[41]

It is easy to overstate the case. There are many of us who have been misled, in past decades, into overstating the case. It was at the nadir, in 1984, that Hugh Hood wrote a hyperbolic introduction to the short story collection *Fatal Recurrences: New Fiction in English from Montreal* that he co-edited with Peter O'Brien:

> Now, suddenly, in the mid-1980s, another surge of creation seems to be peaking here in an extremely diverse body of poetry and, at the same time, an extraordinary amount of new fiction in English, by writers whose first books are just beginning to appear... The final selection was made so as to exhibit as far as possible the extraordinary vitality, variety, and high level of professional accomplishment which distinguishes this new movement, wave, epidemic, outbreak...what's the word?

That was at about the same time that poet van Toorn was talking about "cultural dereliction" and just about a year after novelist T.F. Rigelhof was "sad, lonely, melancholic, chronically depressed" after the publication of his first novel in 1983. Though some of the writers were finding it discouraging, Hood was nonetheless right. There were accomplished writers working in English in Montreal in 1984, and some of them — Anne McLean (aka Ann Diamond), Gail Scott, Jerry Wexler, Robyn Sarah, Edward O. Phillips, Renato Trujillo, H. Nigel Thomas, and Miriam Packer — appeared in his collection.

There are accomplished writers working in English here now, and it can still be discouraging. Being a writer is frequently discouraging, however, no matter where you live. If what has changed is that today it doesn't seem a lot more discouraging in Montreal than anywhere else, that is a considerable change.

The early years I write about here were years in which political activity on the part of Anglo Quebecers had a way of going wrong. Channelling energy into the literary community was a good way of making a difference without bringing the wrath of the nationalists down on our heads.

That changed when the Blue Metropolis Montreal International Literary Festival started making too much of a splash, for we managed to bring some wrath down on our heads in the literary sphere. By that time, though, the landscape was undergoing big changes. We all knew what we were working for, all along. We were working to get noticed. More importantly, we were working to show how a small and unpopular minority could make a contribution to the kind of society most of us — Francophones, Anglophones, and Allophones — wanted to be part of. We had no way of knowing how long it would take — or if all this work would ever bear fruit.

It has borne fruit. If such an amorphous thing as a literary revival can be dated, the seeds for the Anglo Literary Revival were sown with the creation of Blue Metropolis Foundation in 1997 and then of the Quebec Writers' Federation in 1998. The Revival saw the light of day at the inaugural Blue Metropolis Montreal International Literary Festival in 1999 and blossomed over the next two years with the publication of new books by Julie Keith, Ann Charney, and Yann Martel.

Keith's *The Devil Out There* opens with an eponymous novella about a sensible small-town girl at a time of great danger. Having successfully escaped the clutches of her violent father into the arms of her high-school sweetheart, who flushes her birth control pills down the toilet, she lands in a rooming house in the west end of Montreal with a pathetic woman who is in thrall to a young actor who uses his beauty and sensuality to ensnare the unwary. A realist story that makes use of voice, detail and style to fine and chilling effect, "The Devil Out There" is not only imbued with menace but includes criminal activity — cruelty, extortion, rape, murder — that create a link with the genre fiction that so dominated English fiction from Montreal in earlier years. Keith's earlier collection, *The Jaguar Temple and other stories*, was shortlisted for the Governor General's Prize for Fiction in 1995; *The Devil Out There* won the QWF Hugh MacLennan Prize for Fiction and was shortlisted for the Grand Prix du livre de Montréal in 2000.

Charney's *Rousseau's Garden* was passed over for Canadian awards but went on to appear in the United States and in French translation in Quebec and in France, which named her Officier de l'Ordre des Arts et des Lettres. The distance featured in *Rousseau's*

Garden is not generic but geographic. There is no sign of genre fiction in this classic and understated work of realist fiction, but the French setting provides some of the distance that characterized earlier fictions by Montreal's English writers. The first of Charney's works to be set in Montreal is her subsequent novel *Distantly Related to Freud* (2008). This is ironic because the notion of distance figures so prominently, even in the title, of this very Montreal novel. It is also appropriate because the main character, Ellen, whose background has some similarities to Charney's own Polish background, is shown making the crossing from her European roots to a life in Montreal as she moves through her adolescence.

Both generic and geographic distance figure in *Life of Pi*, an imaginative fable in which a young Indian is stranded on a raft with a Royal Bengal tiger until finally reaching the Gulf of Mexico. Yann Martel had emerged as a writer of short fiction in Montreal with *The Facts Behind the Helsinki Roccamatios* in 1993 and then as a novelist with *Self*, in 1996; both books had respectable reviews but disappointing sales. *Life of Pi* was passed over for both the Governor General's Award and the Giller Prize, but won the Quebec Writers' Federation Hugh MacLennan Prize for Fiction — and then, triumphantly, the Booker in 2002.

A magnificent international tribute to Mavis Gallant followed in New York in the fall of 2005, when she also became the first English writer ever to win Quebec's national Prix Athanase-David. Quebec scholars have been taking note of Anglo-Quebec writing to a growing extent since that first colloquium at Université de Montréal in 1997. In 2007 a new history of Quebec literature was published that for the first time acknowledged the existence and the importance of Quebec's English-language writers that paid attention to *littérature anglo-québécoise* — and Blue Metropolis — and included features on Hugh MacLennan, Leonard Cohen, Mordecai Richler, and Mavis Gallant (Biron et al, 2007).

David Homel published *The Speaking Cure* in 2003 and *Midway* in 2010. Edeet Ravel's acclaimed Tel Aviv trilogy consisted of *Ten Thousand Lovers* in 2003, *Look For Me* in 2004, and *A Wall of Light* in 2005. Anita Rau Badami published her third novel, *You Can Hear the Nightbird Call*, in 2006, and Heather O'Neill won Canada Reads and the QWF Prize and was nominated for the Orange Prize

for *Lullabies for Little Criminals* that same year. Louise Penny's first novel, *Still Life*, appeared in London in 2005, followed in remarkably quick succession by *Dead Cold* and *The Cruellest Month* in 2007, *The Murder Stone* in 2008, and *The Brutal Telling* in 2009.

The revival gathered further momentum in 2007 when Neil Smith became Knopf's New Face of Fiction with *Bang Crunch*, and Zoe Whittall published her first novel, *Bottle Rocket Hearts*. *Garcia's Heart*, by Liam Durcan, was among several other notable books published that year. Issa J. Boullata published *A Retired Gentleman and Other Stories* with Banipal Books in London. Peter Behrens won the 2007 Governor General's Award for *The Law of Dreams*, and Rawi Hage's first novel, *De Niro's Game*, was first showcased at Blue Metropolis. Claire Holden Rothman's first novel, *The Heart Specialist*, appeared in 2008, and in that year Miguel Syjuco won the Man Asia Prize for his unpublished first novel *Ilustrado*.

With so many of the international prizewinners overlooked by Canadian judges when they were compiling their shortlists, it is not surprising that some of the best books by Montreal writers have not even been shortlisted for some of the literary awards they should have won. The omission of excellent books by Montreal writers from shortlists and the list of winners of English-Canadian literary prizes is especially characteristic of women writers.

It's cold comfort to know that no one said it would be easy. As a writer, I can sympathize. As a reader, I am glad to know there will always be discoveries to be made that no headline ever trumpeted, for making discoveries is one of the pleasures of reading. As a festival director, I have learned what it takes if you want to make it as a writer. There's no shortcut. The same lessons apply: you need good organizations, you need to keep at it, and you need to make yourself irresistible.

It's hard to judge the extent to which writers now working in English in Montreal see themselves as flourishing, but then this is hard to judge of writers anywhere. Partly this is because we all have different ideas of success and no yardstick at hand. Partly it is because producing a new book takes so much hard work and such a long time that moments of celebration are few and far between.

There are young writers and newcomers to Montreal who have no knowledge of the way things have changed. There are also dozens

of writers here now who have good reason to remember the years of decline, and who understand the difference that we have made.

If we are unlikely to agree on what constitutes literary success, and unlikely to have measured it, it is impossible to establish a causal link between the conditions in which writers work and their eventual success. While the Anglo Literary Revival cannot be seen as the direct result of the creation of any organization or — more plausibly — of a number of different literary organizations and individuals working together, those organizations and individuals have undoubtedly improved the conditions in which writers work and have made their eventual success more likely.

I am just one of those individuals, and Blue Metropolis is only one of those organizations. The Blue Metropolis Festival has been a site for debate and dissent as well as for dialogue and understanding. If its success has been a cause of celebration for some, it has been a cause of resentment for others. The fact that there are limits to its success can itself be a cause of further resentment, as when a writer sells fewer books than he had hoped at his festival launch.

As the largest of the organizations concerned, though, and the one with international reach, there can be no doubt that Blue Metropolis has had a significant impact. It has put English-language writers in touch with one another and with their readers as well as with French-language writers and readers. It has introduced Montreal writers working in French, in English, and in other languages to international publishers, translators, and festival directors, and it has helped put Montreal writers on the international map.

One of the characteristics of the Anglo Literary Revival is its internationalism. It has borne fruit because of international recognition first and foremost, with English Canada coming in with its own honours only after the fact, if at all.

It was the awarding of the Booker Prize in London in 2002 that catapulted Yann Martel to international stardom — and belated recognition in Canada. Edeet Ravel was little known until she found a publisher in London for her Tel Aviv trilogy. Colin McAdam was drawn to my attention when his London publisher, Robin Robertson, mentioned him to me as "the real thing" at the Edinburgh International Book Festival. Louise Penny had been unable to find a publisher for

her first novel, *Still Life*, when she submitted the manuscript for the British Crime Writers' Association's Debut Dagger Award for the best unpublished mystery of the year; when she won second prize, a publication deal with London publisher Hodder Headline followed. She has gone on to win the BCWA's New Blood Award, the Dilys, three Agathas, and the Crime Writers of Canada's Arthur Ellis Award as well as being a finalist for the Barry Award for best mystery/crime novel of the decade.

Jeffrey Moore, who was published by the small press Thistledown Press, was largely unknown until *Prisoner in a Red-Rose Chain* won both the regional and the international Commonwealth Prize in 2000. Madeleine Thien has had recognition both within Canada and internationally, winning the Amazon.ca Books in Canada First Novel Award for her first novel, *Certainty*, which was also a finalist for the Kiriyama Prize in 2006, and in 2010 won the Ovid Festival Prize in Romania. Miguel Syjuco's Man Asia prize for *Ilustrado* preceded his signing a publication contract with Penguin Canada.

The only awards Rawi Hage had won for his first novel, *De Niro's Game*, a year after its publication were the Quebec Writers' Federation Fiction and First Book Prizes. The novel having had only limited success in English Canada, Hage had difficulty placing the book with a Quebec publisher, but it was eventually translated into French as *Parfum de poussière* and published by Éditions Alto in 2008. It took the IMPAC Dublin award to provide the international recognition that has opened subsequent doors.

Hage's second novel, *Cockroach*, was published barely a month later and was nominated for the Giller, the GG and the Rogers; it won the QWF Fiction Prize. *Parfum de poussière* won the Quebec booksellers' Prix des libraires as well as emerging the winner of *Combat des livres*, the Radio-Canada equivalent to *Canada Reads*, where it was successfully championed by English Montreal journalist Brendan Kelly.

If Canadian juries outside of Quebec have been slow to reward Montreal writers working in English, Canadian houses in Toronto and elsewhere have been publishing their work to an unprecedented extent. In some cases this follows international publication, but in other cases the Canadian publisher has recognized Montreal talent

independent of any foreign success. McClelland & Stewart published novels by Neil Bissoondath, George Szanto, and Madeleine Thien, and McArthur and Company has published Edeet Ravel, Louise Penny, Marianne Ackerman, and Kent Stetson.

The same is true of the multinationals. Penguin has published recent work by Colin McAdam, whose second novel *Fall* was nominated for the Giller Prize in 2009, as well as Commonwealth Prize-winner Jeffrey Moore, Man Asia winner Syjuco, and CBC Radio personality Jonathan Goldstein. HarperCollins published early work by David Homel — who has since been published by Douglas & McIntyre and now Cormorant — as well as the novels of Ibi Kaslik and Heather O'Neill. The Montreal writers who have been published by Knopf / Random House include Yann Martel, Edeet Ravel, Will Aitken, Neil Smith, and Kiriyama Prize-winning novelist Anita Rau Badami as well as Julie Keith.

These are the most illustrious cases. Writing remains a difficult task, and being a writer requires not only talent and a measure of luck, but also staying power. Not all who emerge as hopefuls stay the course. Some of the writers who have emerged over the past 15 years — Elyse Gasco won the QWF Prize for her very promising *Can You Wave Bye Bye, Baby?* in 1999 — have written only one book to date. There are some, too, who have either forfeited or acquired a claim to being "Montreal" writers. Yeshim Ternar, Charles Foran, Elisabeth Harvor, Jaspreet Singh, and Denise Roig are among the writers who moved on after years in Montreal. Montreal-born Peter Behrens, who has spent recent years in Maine, published a fine collection of short stories entitled *Night Driving* in 1987 before winning the Governor General's Award for *The Law of Dreams*.

There is no unity among these writers, nothing that could be considered a "school." On the contrary, there are complaints, usually in the name of some higher good, and some of these complaints make it into print. These are liveliest at their most extreme. When Robert Majzels feels misunderstood and under-appreciated, he attacks the community as a whole as well as the commodification of literature (Majzels 2007/2008). David Solway continues to launch vitriolic attacks on writers ranging from the Vehicule poets to Margaret Atwood and Anne Carson as well as on Blue Metropolis (Solway 2002, 2009); T.F. Rigelhof is a writer generous with his praise of

Canadian writers, including many English writers of Montreal, but capable of hostile criticism of writers he does not like (Rigelhof 1990, 2010); and Elias Letelier-Ruz delights in his radical view of literary organizations (2010).[42]

Some of the recent upsurge in literary activity is associated with the creative writing programme in the Concordia University Department of English. Zoe Whittall and Ibi Kaslik are among the Montreal-born writers who moved away after concluding their studies. Liam Durcan, Anita Rau Badami, Madeleine Thien, Johanna Skibsrud, Kathleen Winter, Mikhail Iossel, and Josip Novakovich are among those who have recently moved to Montreal, Iossel and Novakovich in order to teach creative writing at Concordia. Most of the writers mentioned in this book have worked or studied over the years at Concordia, McGill or the Université de Montréal or at one of the five English CÉGEPs.[43]

The eccentricity that characterized English Montreal fiction in the 1980s has not only evolved in the past decade but has itself been recognized in ways hard to imagine in those dark days. *Life of Pi* is, after all, a fable. Trevor Ferguson moved into crime fiction in 1999 with *City of Ice*, which was published under the name of John Farrow in order to prevent publishers from learning the low sales figures of his earlier novels; the result was international publication and a six-figure advance. In addition to Louise Penny's crime fiction, there is a substantial amount of other genre fiction written by such Montreal writers as Michael Blair (thriller), John Brooke (crime), A.J. Gillard (romance), Wendy MacIntyre (historical romance), and Claude Lalumière (science fiction).

When it comes to experimentation, some of the writers innovating in recent books are the same ones doing so in earlier periods.[44] With Atwood herself experimenting in much of her recent work not only with historical fiction and science or speculative fiction, experimentation in Canadian writing can hardly be distinguished from work considered mainstream. The novels of such successful writers as Martel, Siblin, and Syjuco are surely experimental by any definition, even if they are also popular successes. It might be argued that mainstream work now commonly includes experimentation, or perhaps that experimentation has gone mainstream, which are arguments that could be made of the work of such Montreal writers as Maya Merrick, Louis Rastelli, Daniel

Allen Cox, spoken word artist Catherine Kidd, and genre-bending poet Anne Carson.

Like Canadian writing — and Quebec writing — in general, Montreal writing is characterized by great diversity. This is not a new phenomenon. There were gay writers here in the 1980s — Gail Scott, Edward O. Phillips, H. Nigel Thomas, and Will Aitken among them — and there are gay writers here today, including those same writers as well as newcomers like Peter Dubé, Daniel Allen Cox, Nairne Holtz, and Elise Moser. Montreal was home in the 1980s to the imaginative Turkish novelist and essayist Yeshim Ternar and Chilean immigrant Renato Trujillo; Pakistani-Canadian Julian Samuel, and Italian-Canadian Michael Mirolla were also publishing fiction at the time, when there was limited interest in their work. St. Vincent-born writer H. Nigel Thomas's first novel, *Spirits in the Dark*, was not only published by House of Anansi Press in 1993 and shortlisted for a QWF Fiction Prize, but went on to appear as part of Heinemann's prestigious Caribbean Writers series.

Issa J. Boullata is a Palestinian born in Jerusalem, and Dimitri Nasrallah and Rawi Hage are Lebanese. Rana Bose, Jaspreet Singh, Saleema Nawaz, and Anita Rau Badami have Indian roots, while those of Neil Bissoondath, H. Nigel Thomas, and Kaie Kellough are in the Caribbean. Akhtar Naraghi is Iranian; Licia Canton was born in Italy; Pan Bouyoucas (who writes in French as well as in English) and Tess Fragoulis have their roots in Greece; and Miguel Syjuco is from the Philippines. What has changed is less the proportion of writers with their roots in other cultures than the far greater national and international interest shown today in the work of such writers.

The Véhicule Fiction Series, now edited by Andrew Steinmetz, who is himself a distinguished novelist as well as a poet and essayist, includes award-winning books by Liam Durcan, Rana Bose and Jaspreet Singh, as well as Ann Charney's *Rousseau's Garden*. DC Books continues to publish fiction, now under the Punchy imprint directed by Jason Camlot and David McGimpsey, including a first novel by Arjun Basu. The ranks of Anglo literary presses publishing fiction have been swelled by Andy Brown's Conundrum Press, Longbridge Books, which is owned by Domenic Cusmano, and Jon Paul Fiorentino's Snare Books, as well as Guernica, recently returned to Montreal under the ownership of

Connie McParland and Michael Mirolla. Robin Philpot has reinvented himself as the English-language publisher of Baraka Books. The kind of publishing activity that was seen in Toronto in the 1960s and 1970s is finally taking place in Montreal half a century later on.

Many Montreal writers working in English rely on small and medium-sized presses in Ontario and the rest of Canada, including House of Anansi (H. Nigel Thomas, Rawi Hage, Peter Behrens, Eric Siblin, Kathleen Winter), Coach House (Gail Scott), Insomniac (David McGimpsey, Louis Rastelli, Jon Paul Fiorentino), Goose Lane Editions (Colleen Curran), Arsenal Pulp Press (Daniel Allen Cox, Ami Sands Brodoff), Freehand Books (Saleema Nawaz), Oberon Press (Mary Soderstrom, T.F. Rigelhof, Claire Rothman, David Manicom), Porcupine's Quill (Joel Yanofsky), Second Story Press (Ami Sands Brodoff), Mercury Press (Robert Majzels, Gail Scott), NeWest (Alice Zorn), TSAR (H. Nigel Thomas, Rana Bose), and Gaspereau Press (Johanna Skibsrud).

Signature Editions, founded in Montreal as Nuage Editions in 1986 and based in Winnipeg since the late 1990s, has published fiction by Julie Keith (the GG-shortlisted *The Jaguar Temple and Other Stories*) as well as Edeet Ravel, Denise Roig, John Brooke, Linda Ghan, and me. Under Jan and Gary Geddes and then Jan Geddes alone, Cormorant has a long tradition of publishing English writers from Montreal, including Nino Ricci, who won the Governor General's Award for Fiction for *Lives of the Saints* (1990) and Claudia Morrison, author of a first-person historical novel, *From the Foot of the Mountain* (2000) set in Pompeii immediately before it was obliterated in the eruption of Mount Vesuvius.[45] Cormorant has continued this tradition under new owner Marc Côté, who has published recent novels by Neil Bissoondath, Ann Charney, David Homel, Elise Moser, Claire Holden Rothman, Mary Soderstrom, and Zoe Whittall.

The renaissance of Anglo fiction may have peaked by now, or it may not yet have peaked. We may still be waiting for the great writer, as for the Messiah, or we may not still be waiting for the great writer. It might be that it will turn out to be a writer already publishing. It's too soon to tell how their reputations and those of other writers will weather the passage of time. And who can tell what great book might even now be slouching towards Toronto — or New York, or London — to be born?

Francophone Quebecers have been showing increased interest in English-language writers and greater acceptance of their place in Quebec literature. The greatest sign of this move towards greater openness is that on November 8, 2006, Mavis Gallant finally won the Prix du Québec for literature, the Prix Athanase-David.

It was at the Université de Montréal colloquium in 1997 that I first suggested it was time that Mavis Gallant win the Prix Athanase-David. Gallant is a great Quebec writer who is largely unrecognized within Quebec. She is not only Montreal-born, with a unique experience of both French and English Montreal, but the author of what I consider to be the finest stories ever written about the Montreal of the 1920s and the 1940s and some of the finest fiction written by anyone, in any language, on the personal meaning and after-effects of World War II. She is undoubtedly a worthy recipient, and if she wrote in French she would have won the prize many years ago.

The other Prix du Québec had already gone to English-speaking Quebecers in other disciplines both artistic and scientific. There have been winners of the Prix Athanase-David itself who are immigrants to Quebec — Monique Bosco and Naïm Kattan — and who work in French. Language and literature are so significantly linked with Quebec's sense of itself as a nation that the Prix Athanase-David has been the holy of holies. There was something heretical in 1997 about suggesting that an English-language writer should win the Prix Athanase-David.

For Gallant to win would, though, send a signal that writers working in English are part of Quebec literature. That there is a place for us in Quebec literature and, indeed, that there can be such a thing as *littérature anglo-québécoise*. That it is time, all these decades after the Quiet Revolution, to redefine what is meant by Quebec literature in such a way as to include writers who work in English as well as immigrant writers.

I was involved in nominating Mavis Gallant for the Prix Athanase-David on two different occasions, in 1999 and in 2002, and she won on neither of those occasions. When the Quebec Writers' Federation proposed nominating her again, in 2006, she was understandably reluctant to have her name put forward for a third time. All of us interested in the future of Quebec literature have reason to be glad that she did agree to do so.

The importance of having an English-speaking juror should not be underestimated, and here the Quebec Writers' Federation has played a role in lobbying to raise the profile of English writing and in proposing jurors likely to appreciate books written in English. Julie Keith's second collection of fiction, *The Devil Out There*, was shortlisted for the Grand Prix du livre de Montréal. The fact that Ann Charney was on the jury for the Prix Athanase-David in 2006 was critical in Gallant's win, and it is hard to imagine that the Grand Prix du livre de Montréal would have gone to English Montreal poet David Solway in 2004 if it had not been for the presence of Richard King on the jury.

I was in a foreign place — Budapest — when I wrote my first novel, living in a language not my own and struggling with disconcerting customs and manners. I have great respect for the effect of place on a writer — and even for the effect of a non-place, for Anglo Montreal had become a non-place by the time I was emerging on to the literary scene. The story I have told is the story of the re-creation of Montreal, and there are lots of lessons here, and not only for Montrealers. There are lessons here for anyone who has a Toronto in their life.

I learned some of these lessons the hard way, through personal experience. But when I had learned enough of them, I realized there were other literary contexts I could have learned from, as well. Women's writing is the most obvious example of a writing that was languishing in obscurity and that has pulled itself up by its own bootstraps in recent decades. I knew this history; I had followed it all my professional life, and it helped to illuminate the situation of English Quebec writers when we ourselves had started to emerge from obscurity.

It's only in the past couple of years that I have been able to see the relevance of the Anglo-Irish Literary Revival to Anglo Montreal. That was an insight that had to await the past decade, for it was premature even to think in terms of a revival until it had started to happen. It is a revelation that was then inspired by reading the Irish historian R.F. Foster's biography of William Butler Yeats. When the student is ready, the teacher appears.

This is what we had been working for, without having any way of knowing it would ever happen. Like the fall of the Berlin Wall,

it was something that seemed obvious only in retrospect. Not even the dissidents in Eastern Europe had the slightest idea, just weeks beforehand, that momentous change was around the corner.

We are all winners in a literary revival: other writers, publishers, translators, readers, the entire literary milieu out of which writers emerge and flourish, and society at large. No literary revival is likely to have the impact of the fall of the Berlin Wall. The very fact that we managed to turn around so unpromising a literary context, though, is reason for rejoicing and for hope. It's also a tale worth telling. If we could do it, others can, too, in other literary contexts, in other contexts.

There are lessons in this story for every writer who hankers for recognition, no matter what their gender, language, background, or nationality. There are lessons for every Canadian who has indulged in Toronto bashing, and there are lessons for writers envious of Margaret Atwood. There are lessons for every place writers come from, which means there are lessons here for every place. I have a great respect for the effect that writers can have on the world they live in.

I have had a great deal to say about Montreal, which I know well, and relatively little to say about Toronto, which I do not know well. But Toronto informs this story from beginning to end. Toronto has been a source of frustration, and it has been a source of inspiration, as well, both during my very first visits there and in ways that have taken me half a lifetime to appreciate. Without Toronto, the story I have told would be an entirely different story. If there hadn't been a Toronto, we would have to have invented Toronto. Perhaps we did.

Canadian nationalism emerged in the 1960s and steamed through the 1970s and 1980s. Its bible was George Grant's *Lament for a Nation* (1965), and its calling card was Margaret Atwood's *Survival: A Thematic Guide to Canadian Literature* (1970), a book focused on English-Canadian writing that has just one chapter devoted to writing in French. Canadian nationalism peaked with the spike in Toronto's economic influence and has faded with the rise of Calgary as a populist powerhouse with little interest in culture except to the extent that it pays its own way.

Quebec nationalism has deeper roots and more staying power, even if old stock Quebec Francophones' sense of their own identity

underwent a seismic shift after the death of Maurice Duplessis and the Quiet Revolution as the province of "Canadiens," "Canadiens français," and the Roman Catholic Church became associated with "Québécois" and the French language of Quebec. Quebec nationalism is a volcano that could erupt again on short notice, as it has done several times before. The usual proximate cause is a perceived insult to Quebec's language and identity in challenges to the Charter of the French Language, for example, or in video footage of English Canadians trampling the Quebec flag. This is a dangerous country for flags.

Whatever lies in store for Quebec nationalism — and Canadian nationalism — there are new challenges ahead for Montreal's English-language writers. One of the changes affecting artists everywhere in Canada is the election in 2006 of a Conservative government, which is less committed to culture than were recent Liberal governments. With the Anglo Literary Revival so dependent on international exposure, it is possible that the cuts to the touring programmes funded through the Department of Foreign Affairs and International Trade as "PromArt" will have a worse impact on us than on other Canadian artists.

The power base of Quebec nationalism is rural, conservative Quebec — Bloc country, Péquiste country, and sometimes Conservative country — but most of its battles are fought in Montreal. It is in Montreal that the English language is most used, and the English language is sometimes perceived as a threat to the future of Quebec and the survival of the French language. It is in Montreal that most of Quebec's English speakers live, and we are often viewed as another threat.

And it is in Montreal that the federally supported idea of bilingualism has some of the strongest support in the country. Montreal's Anglophones tend to view bilingualism as a protection for their own community and generally see bilingualism as a positive thing; many of them just wish they were more bilingual. Sovereignists often view bilingualism as a menace to the future of French.

This can occasionally make life difficult for outspoken English Montrealers. We may speak French fluently. This will take us so far, but no further, unless we choose to live our lives in French and "pass" as Francophones — which is a choice that some Montrealers have made.

Most of us carry a lot of Anglo baggage around with us, whether or not the baggage belongs to us. The fact that we speak English sets us apart. The lines are drawn; these lines may never be quite straight, they don't often matter much, but they are drawn all the same, and in some real sense, even today, we Anglo Montrealers remain "Other." We are not supposed to speak up, and certainly not to criticize, as the bilingual filmmaker Jacob Tierney learned the hard way when he criticized Quebec cinema for not being inclusive (McPherson 2010).

These are the rival nationalisms that have dominated our political and cultural discourse over the past half-century. The federal government, which might play the role of referee between English-Canadian and Quebec nationalism — between Toronto and Montreal — is inevitably brought into play in some of the brawls, especially over language, especially in Quebec. The federal government is, after all, the government of Canada, and the battle is over what Canada is and what Canada means.

Like many battles, this is a battle that cannot be won. What matters is coping with complexity, with one another. What matters is just muddling along, as we have always done.

It's the fact that we've been able to do that that makes this an amazing place, an idea we hang on to stubbornly, against all reason, without quite knowing what we mean by it. It was about 25 years ago that I became active in Montreal's English-language literary milieu, and when I did so it was in order to make it more likely that a writer working here in English could thrive and contribute to the society we live in. It was 14 years ago that I started thinking about Blue Metropolis — first as a magazine, then as a festival — as one of the essentials for a thriving literary community and a society open to all.

The work is not done — it will never be done — but I have done what I can do. I have given thought to leaving Blue Metropolis in the past, for the work has been gruelling as well as exciting. When I decided in the last days of 2009 that I would resign and give the organization a year to figure out how best to proceed, I did so knowing that change is vital and necessary, not only for an individual, for me, but also for an organization.

I had written most of this book before then, and I have spent some of the intervening time revising the manuscript. This hasn't been easy, for writing is never easy. It felt right, though, to do it in

the throes of preparations for my last festival, while simultaneously organizing the Blue Metropolis Translation Slam as the only literary event at the Canadian Pavilion at Shanghai's World Expo 2010. With my colleagues I have also been developing a partnership with the Luminato Festival in Toronto for a preview of the Chinese Slam and working on the international promotion of Francophone Quebec writings in Words Without Borders, as well as setting in motion half a dozen other literary and educational programmes for young people. As I write, in other words, I am working in the present on projects that will stand Blue Metropolis well in the future even as I am looking back on the past out of which Blue Metropolis emerged.

So what can be hoped for of the Anglo Literary Revival? Among the benefits are respect, recognition, awards, and honours, all of which were lacking in the mid-1980s. These are important not only to individual writers but to the English-speaking community as a whole because they create a sense of pride, of value, and of identity, all of which have been in short supply in English-speaking Montreal in recent decades. They can also inspire new writers with a wish to add their own voices and have their own say, adding to the variety and richness of the community in the process. Whether or not the Anglo Literary Revival produces a genius, that one great figure we will all recognize as standing head and shoulders above the others, its writers have already made people across the world sit up and take notice. There is no better tonic for any community.

In the case of Quebec, which until just a few years ago defined Quebec literature with writing in French only and rejected the very notion of a *littérature anglo-québécoise*, the resurgence of English writing from Montreal has an even more significant impact. It poses a challenge to the prevalent view of Quebec as French-only — and it does so without opposing any language law or threatening anyone's livelihood, without waving any flag and without casting a ballot for any political option.

For the Anglo Literary Revival is not a political movement. This should go without saying, but I think it worth saying, for I have good reason to wonder if anything in Quebec can ever be untouched by politics. The Anglo Literary Revival includes writers who are federalists, writers who are *indépendantistes*, and writers who are neither.

It includes writers who are recent arrivals, writers who will be here for only a few years, and writers whose families have lived in Quebec for centuries. It includes writers from the radical political fringe and writers from the political centre, Israeli writers and Palestinian writers, Indian writers and Pakistani writers, Iraqi writers and American writers, not to mention Catholic writers and Protestant writers, Jewish writers, Muslim writers, and Hindu writers. It includes writers so different in their backgrounds, cultures, religions, races, countries of origin, styles, genres, and interests that it's hard to imagine it being harnessed for any political purpose.

It includes those who have been written about in the academy and those who have never been written about in the academy. It includes Francophile Anglo writers suspicious of Blue Metropolis because it promotes Montreal's English-language writers along with Francophones; it includes Anglo writers (these are sometimes the very same Francophile writers) who are resentful that Blue Metropolis has not done more to promote them and their work. It includes writers who have a gift for promoting themselves and writers who have no such gift — and, in some cases, no such interest. It includes writers whose main goal is to make a living as a writer and writers who have no interest in how many copies their books sell. It includes some who don't like even the idea of an Anglo Literary Revival.

It is not only diverse and companionable, but also quarrelsome and unpredictable. The Anglo Literary Revival is just about as various as the society in which we all live, here in Montreal, and the writers who are part of the Revival have only one thing in common, and that is that they write in English. Whatever Quebec chooses as its political future, the Anglo Literary Revival proposes a more inclusive understanding of Quebec literature than we have seen. In so doing, it also proposes a more inclusive understanding of Quebec society.

If that is political, then our very existence as writers working in English in Montreal is political. And of course it is — and not only for Quebec. Our very existence as writers working in English in Montreal is a reminder to English Canada that Canadian literature and Quebec literature are not two different literatures.

It was in the aftermath of the 1995 Referendum that Lise Bissonnette wrote about English-speaking artists and intellectuals in places not often visited by the traditional elites. It was the intellectuals

and artists, she reminded her readers, who prepared the way for the Quiet Revolution. The intellectuals and artists of the 1940s and 1950s that she is referring to are those associated with Paul-Émile Borduas and Refus global. What makes her editorial so remarkable even today — as it certainly was in 1996 — is that she allows for the possibility that English-speaking artists and intellectuals could have a similar impact:

> Underground and little known, in places not often visited by the traditional elites, these [intellectuals and artists] again are the ones who sense how Quebec will change when it fully accepts its pluralism. Instead of rejecting them, as in the past, we should be encouraging them to speak up.[46]

Many of the writers of English Montreal still hang out underground, in places not often visited by the traditional elite, like the Yellow Door Coffee House on Aylmer Street and the bars on The Main. There are many, too, who have come up for air and who can be found across town at the Lion d'or every November for the Quebec Writers' Federation's annual gala — and in the Delta Centre-Ville Hotel during Blue Metropolis at the end of April. These writers are the ones who sense how Quebec will change when it fully accepts its pluralism.

- fin -

NOTES

[1] A July 9, 2010 communiqué from the Writers' Union of Canada, the Professional Writers Association of Canada, the Playwrights Guild of Canada, and the League of Canadian Poets describes these as the "four leading professional organizations representing Canadian writers" without making any reference to Union des écrivaines et des écrivains québécois. Academic publication is both more careful and more correct, and scholarly journals such as Canadian Literature and Studies in Canadian Literature include writing in French as well as writing in English (and, very occasionally, in other languages). Many academic titles (e.g. Gadpaille 1989; Nischik, ed. 2007) nonetheless use "Canadian" to refer only to work in English.

[2] Return of the Sphinx was treated with respect by American critics, but MacLennan's reputation in Canada never recovered (Cameron 1981, 332-5).

[3] "Montreal's 'third force' — the non-Francophone, non-Anglophone minorities — has been labeled in different ways through the twentieth century. They have been called Neo-Canadians, Néo-Québécois, Allophones, and, more recently, 'Cultural Communities' and 'Ethnic Minorities'" (Levine 1990, x).

[4] Simon Harel writes that "les lettres anglo-québécoises sont avant tout montréalaises" (2007/2008, 49), though he himself prefers to use the broader term, as I did when I first wrote on the subject in the 1980s. I have chosen now to focus on Montreal, for this book is in part a memoir, and I can only write about what I know. There are undoubtedly similarities between writers working in Montreal and those working elsewhere in Quebec as regards language and invisibility, but there are differences, too, and I don't want to downplay those. There appears to be much less (if any) stigma attached to being a member of the English-speaking community in Quebec City, for example, than is the case in Montreal. There are advantages to living in Montreal, however, and these are keenly felt in the regions. These advantages have become more pronounced since the advent of literary organizations based in Montreal, of a festival that takes place in the city, and other signs of urban cultural vitality that have not yet provided significant benefits to writers in the regions. All this said, I should add that it is impossible to draw a clear line between region and metropolis, given that so many fiction writers associated with the regions are also Montreal writers. They include Hugh MacLennan, Mordecai Richler, Louise Penny, and Robert Allen dividing their time between Montreal and the Townships, Jeffrey Moore in the Laurentians, Kenneth Radu in Senneville and later St. Polycarpe, former Montrealer Neil Bissoondath in Quebec City, H. Nigel Thomas in Quebec City and now Montreal, and John Lavery in Gatineau.

[5] When the context is hockey, *Canadiens* always refers to the Montreal Canadiens. In general Montreal has its own lexicon. Writing in 1990, Levine (x) described the vocabulary used to denote Montreal's language groups as "bewildering" to those not familiar with the city and its linguistic divisions. "The English-speaking community is variously described as English-speakers, Anglophones, and English Canadians. Similarly, the French-speaking community is referred to as "French-speakers," "Francophones," and "French-Canadians" or "French Québécois." "English-speaking Community" is the designation used of the Official-language Minority of Quebec by the Government of Canada. Some of the writers I consulted in the course of my research (Leith 1989) rejected the use of "English," some preferred "Anglo" to "Anglophone," and some rejected both of these terms. Jason Camlot suggests that the use of "Anglo" rather than "English" represents "a significant shift since the 1970s in ideas about Englishness and linguistic identity in Quebec" (Camlot 2007). These are issues of identity that continue to be disputed; see Harel's comment comparing "l'Anglo nouveau" to "le Beaujolais du même nom" (2007/2008, 52).

[6] According to the 2006 census, 575,555 (7.6 per cent of the population) in Quebec declare English as their only mother tonguge, 744,430 (10 per cent) use mostly English as their home language, and 918,955 (12.2 per cent) comprise the Official-language Minority, having English as their First Official language spoken (Statistics Canada, 2006). Jedwab (2008) discusses the different criteria used by the federal government and the government of Quebec in their definitions of English-speaking Quebecers.

[7] My focus throughout this book is on fiction writers, though I do comment on poets (Layton, Klein, Gustafson, and later Robert Allen and Elisabeth Harvor) who are also writers of fiction and on poets whose situation differed from that of fiction writers of the time (as was the case with the Vehicule poets in the 1970s). Some comments on the literary scene made by Endre Farkas, Peter van Toorn, and other poets and anthologists apply not only to poets but to all Montreal writers.

[8] Mavis Gallant's last visit to Montreal was in 2002, when she won the Blue Metropolis Montreal International Literary Grand Prix. One of the events included was an on-stage conversation about the Montreal of the 1940s between Gallant and her old friend William Weintraub, for which he proposed the title: "The Good Old Bad Old Days."

[9] John Ralston Saul distinguishes between positive nationalism and negative nationalism, and classifies this Canadian nationalism as positive, which is also the way he sees the first Parti Québécois government of 1976 (Saul 1997, 304). The distinction between positive and negative surely

depends in some part on what group one belongs to. Naturally enough, Quebec nationalists see their own project in positive terms; some of them consider the Official-languages Act and bilingualism — which in 1999 UNEQ president Denise Boucher memorably described at our meeting as "*une vision frankscottienne*" — as a threat to the survival of French in Quebec.

10 Political scientist Daniel Salée wrote in 1977 of non-Francophone Quebecers that "they are strangers in their own house... They are invited to partake in *la nation québécoise* but according to terms and parameters upon which they have little or no control. They can be in the nation, if they wish; somehow, they will never really be of the nation" (1977, 9).

11 Theoretical support for authorial independence is provided by Gilles Deleuze and Félix Guattari in their work on minor literatures: "*Si l'écrivain reste en marge ou à l'écart de sa communauté fragile, cette situation le met d'autant plus en mesure d'exprimer une autre communauté potentielle, de forger les moyens d'une autre conscience et d'une autre sensibilité.*" Deleuze and Guattari, 1975, 28-29; translation 1986 by Dana Polan, 17: "If the writer is in the margins or completely outside his or her fragile community, this situation allows the writer all the more the possibility to express another possible community and to forge the means for another consciousness and another sensibility."

12 If the story of the poetry written in English by Montreal writers is similar in some ways to that of the fiction, literary non-fiction has a different history, with certain writers — Sheila McLeod Arnopoulos and Dominique Clift, Charles Taylor, Witold Rybczynski, Merrily Weisbord, and Elaine Kalman Naves, as well as Josh Freed and Jon Kalina — having success with books published in otherwise hard literary times. The international success of more recent non-fiction by such writers as Mark Abley, Taras Grescoe, Cleo Paskal, and of my son Adam Leith Gollner coincides with the revival in fiction writing.

13 "*Dans la mesure où l'équation langue/nation/identité est toujours à l'avant-plan, dès qu'il est question de valider la singularité des lettres québécoises, l'expression littéraire anglo-québécoise est encore un fait marginal.*" / English-language writing in Quebec will remain marginal for as long as the language/nation/identity equation is important — and for as long as we have to justify the specificity of Quebec literature (Harel 1998-1999, 47). Here and throughout, otherwise uncredited translations are my own.

14 Ipsos Reid poll February 23, 2010 (www.ipsos.com [website]).

15 As quoted by Bloc Québécois leader Gilles Duceppe to Canadian Press on 5 April 2010.

16 Leith, 1987.

[17] There were exceptions, especially between working class English-speaking and Francophone Catholics, and occasionally in more privileged families. Mavis Gallant, however, was one of the very few English-speaking Protestant children of her generation (she was born in 1922) to have been sent to a French Catholic school.

[18] As philosopher Charles Taylor has said, "Big business spoke English" (1993, 166).

[19] I have written about this period in *Marrying Hungary* (2008).

[20] Statistics Canada 1971–2001.

[21] There are two notable Canadian writers named Charles Taylor, one of whom is the Toronto essayist (1935–1997) after whom the Charles Taylor Prize for Literary Non-fiction is named; the other is the Montreal philosopher born in 1931.

[22] Statistics Canada, 1971–2001. These figures are of Anglophones whose mother tongue is English; for those for whom English is the language most often spoken at home, the population change was from 886,100 in 1971 to 746,898 in 2001, i.e. 139,000 people.

[23] See http://kimmcgowan.blogspot.com/2010/02/dissertation-narrative-mode-and-being.html [website] for good-natured posts from members of the Jealous-of-Margaret-Atwood Club.

[24] "Montreal's linguistic upheaval was a cardinal development in Canadian political history, inextricably linked to the country's national unity crises of the 1960s and 1970s" (Levine 5). "The linguistic and cultural compromises that will be realized over the next few years in the Montreal area... will ultimately determine the manner in which the French majority considers its relations with the rest of Canada" (Arnopoulos and Clift).

[25] Issues of identity are raised by the number of other Anglo Montreal writers who have changed the names under which they write. Endre (formerly André) Farkas, Yeshim (formerly Yesim) Ternar, Erin Moure (also Erín Moure, formerly Erin Mouré), Sheila McLeod Arnopoulos (also Sheila Arnopoulos), Julie Keith (formerly Julie Houghton Keith), and Claire Holden Rothman (formerly Claire Rothman) are others who have changed the names under which they publish for a variety of personal reasons. Playwright and prose writer David Fennario (né Wiper) has used his pen name in all his productions and publications, as has fiction writer Fran Ponomarenko, who writes under the name Ludmilla Bereshko; novelist Trevor Ferguson made a conscious break with his previous publishing history when he began publishing as John Farrow in 1999. The possibility of

a link between these issues of identity and those mentioned above (see note 5) is suggestive in a literary milieu uncertain of its identity and its standing in Canadian literature.

26 Scott's narrator does not choose to go to McGill, but does so only because her "surrealist coin" falls on the Roddick Gates during a game that involves tossing coins on to a map of Montreal and then going to the location: "Ugh, English Montreal. Reluctantly I go over. The Waspies have just stepped from their student cover to enjoy the spring. They sit in loose jeans and humped backs under huge sweaters on the stone fence. As if their little pea heads were the only bodily part that worked" (Scott 1987, 76).

27 Véhicule Press takes an accent, but none is used for the Vehicule poets.

28 CJAD Radio [Montreal], August 1989.

29 Novelist Robert Majzels considers himself a member of "a small minority within the English-speaking minority" (Majzels 2007/2008, 66), and poet Elias Letelier-Ruz distances himself from Anglo literary institutions (2010).

30 Nepveu's notes for the 1997 conference are reproduced in Moyes 2007/2008 (3). Academic interest in Anglo-Quebec writing within Quebec has developed since the 1997 colloquium, when few Francophone scholars responded to a call for papers (Moyes 2007/2008, 1) and now includes some Francophones as well as Anglophones; the English-language fiction writers these scholars have shown the greatest interest in are Gail Scott and Robert Majzels, who are among the English-language writers who have chosen to distance themselves from English-speaking Montreal. There is belated interest in the work of Mordecai Richler (as noted by Harel 2007/2008, 49), but little interest to date in other contemporary fiction writers working in English.

31 In French, the question on the ballot asked: "*Acceptez-vous que le Québec devienne souverain, après avoir offert formellement au Canada un nouveau partenariat économique et politique, dans le cadre du projet de loi sur l'avenir du Québec et de l'entente signée le 12 juin 1995?*" ("Do you agree that Québec should become sovereign after having made a formal offer to Canada for a new economic and political partnership within the scope of the bill respecting the future of Québec and of the agreement signed on June 12, 1995?"). For the Projet de la loi sur la souveraineté du *Québec*, see http://www.ncf.ca/ip/newspaper/ledroit/services/loi.pq [website].

32 "*S'il importe de comprendre ce que 'nous' sommes, de faire appel au passé pour mieux expliciter les relations tendues avec le voisinage' anglophone, la reconnaissance récente des lettres anglo-québécoises est un profond signe de*

changement" (If it's a question of understanding who *we* are, of looking to the past to understand difficult relations with our Anglophone 'neighbours,' the recent recognition of Anglo-Quebec literature is an important sign of change"). Harel 2007/2008, 48.

[33] The letter is dated March 3, 1999 and is copied to the three arts councils with funding we had applied to.

[34] Dion had angered sovereignists with his letters to *Le Devoir* in 1996-97 and in the "Clarity Act," wherein the Canadian government aimed to impose rules pertaining to any future referendum on independence.

[35] A copy of the letter was sent to Denise Boucher. The letter of cancellation sent by Hélène Pelletier-Baillargeon on March 8, 1999 says that she had just returned from a trip to discover faxed copies of letters exchanged between UNEQ and Blue Metropolis.

[36] "*Metropolis bleu qui sert bien les objectifs de bilinguisme et de biculturalisme du gouvernement fédéral.*"

[37] "*L'argent, c'est le nerf de la guerre. On assiste à une vraie bataille de subventions. Si Metropolis bleu demande une somme d'argent aux instances gouvernementales et que l'UNEQ en demande autant, qui va sortir gagnant?*"

[38] "*S'il y avait un questionnement, dans cette ville de festivals censés être uniques à chaque discipline… ce serait dans la mesure où il porterait ombrage, question de financement toujours, à l'autre festival international de littérature.*"

[39] "*On voit que la situation dans laquelle se trouvaient les travailleurs francophones au début des années 1970, qui avait amené les auteurs de l'énonce de politique de 1977 (loi 101) à en faire une 'question de justice sociale' a été largement corrigée, ce qui peut être attribué aussi à d'autres facteurs que la Charte.*" Québec, 1996, 70-71; quoted in Floch and Pocock, 2008 (their translation), 36.

[40] See R.F. Foster's analysis of the decline of the Anglo-Irish Ascendancy and the literary effects of nationalism in Ireland in Volume 1 of his magnificent biography *W.B. Yeats: The Apprentice Mage*.

[41] "In my working life," Lori Schubert wrote, "I have been frustrated when Canadian opinion-makers failed to notice how many of the country's finest English-language writers are based here in Quebec. So imagine my combined state of delight and disappointment to see not one, not two, but three world-class writers with significant ties to Quebec reviewed in the June 13 Book Review with nary a mention of the province due north of Manhattan. Anne Carson and Jaspreet Singh each spent years living and writing in Montreal, and Miguel Syjuco (referred to in Raymond Bonner's review as living in 'North America')

has lived and worked here for the last three years. This is not a reproach — the three reviewers could hardly have picked up on the coincidence — but I felt I had to seize this opportunity to let the rest of 'North America' (and the world) know that Quebec, often seen as a purely French cultural centre, in fact harbours a thriving English language literary community." The full text of her letter to the *New York Times Book Review*, Sunday, June 27, 2010 is reprinted in the *Montreal Review of Books*, Spring 2010, 10.

[42] For an exploration of some of the issues of conflict relating to English Quebec writing, see Harel 2007/2008.

[43] In his introduction to *Fatal Recurrences* (1984), Hugh Hood, who was a Université de Montréal faculty member, notes the number of contributors (including H. Nigel Thomas and Miriam Packer) associated with *Études anglaises*, a department with which Gail Scott has been associated in recent years. Concordia faculty members from Clark Blaise to Elizabeth Spencer and Terence Byrnes especially have played determining role in their students' careers, and the many individuals associated with Concordia who have played roles in publishing English writers of Quebec include Gary Geddes, Robert Allen, Karen Haughian, and Jon Paul Fiorentino, while Stephanie Bolster has been active in publicizing literary activity and Mikhail Iossel in bringing Summer Literary Seminars to Montreal. Writers who have worked or studied at McGill include not only Hugh MacLennan, Louis Dudek, A.M. Klein, Constance Beresford-Howe, Leonard Cohen, Bharati Mukherjee, and George Szanto, but countless more recent faculty members and alumni; in publishing the role of McGill Queen's University Press, Robert Lecker's ECW Press, and that of former McGill student Marc Côté's Cormorant Books should be noted. The universities play a significant role in drawing writers to Montreal and fostering them, even if only for a few years, and thus contributing to the literary activity of the city. The English CÉGEPs have contributed significant writers, including T.F. Rigelhof, Will Aitken, and Michael Harris at Dawson; Claire Holden Rothman and Monique Polak at Marianopolis; Keith Henderson, Steve Luxton, and Fran Ponomarenko at Vanier; and Robyn Sarah at Champlain, with John Abbott notable for a very literary English department that has included Claudia Lapp, Endre Farkas, Claudia Morrison, David Solway, Peter van Toorn, Lori Weber, Edeet Ravel, Susan Gillis, and Kenneth Radu, and others.

[44] Majzels dismisses "experimental writing," which "has become a harmlessly clever entertainment"; he retains an interest in "particular experiments" (2007/2008, 66, 68).

[45] Morrison lived in Pointe-Claire on the West Island of Montreal and, like Hugh Hood, spent summers in Eastern Ontario.

[46] Bissonnette wrote, "*Partout à Montréal, sur les campus, dans les galéries et musées, chez les musiciens et artistes de la scène, chez les écrivains et traducteurs, dans les publications culturelles parallèles, des Québécois de langue anglaise ont perdu intérêt aux querelles politiques des corps constitués et les impasses où se sont enfoncés leurs aînés. Ils ne sont pas souverainistes pour autant, cela n'a d'ailleurs aucune importance, mais ils vivent pleinement ici pour y rester, ils sont en prise sur l'ensemble des milieux de réflexion et de création, ils ont attachés au Québec tel qu'il est et surtout tel qu'il pourrait devenir s'ils s'y sentaient un rôle plus déterminant. Ce sont les milieux intellectuels et culturels qui, au cours des années quarante et cinquante, ont préparé la voie à la révolution tranquille. Ce sont encore ceux qui, de façon souterraine et méconnue, dans des lieux peu fréquentés par les élites traditionnelles, devinent l'inévitable mutation de la société québécoise quand elle aura pleinement accepté son pluralisme. Plutôt que les rejeter, comme autrefois, il faut les amener à parler plus fort*" (Bissonnette, 1996).

[47] This Bibliography of English Montreal fiction is not exhaustive, and the criteria for inclusion are necessarily fluid, given the vagaries of writers' lives. The writers included work or worked in English in the post-war period. Most are associated with Montreal, a few with other regions of Quebec (see note 5), and with few exceptions the books listed are professionally published (as opposed to being self-published). There are writers whose association with Montreal is so significant that they should be considered Montreal writers no matter where they happen to live; I include Mavis Gallant, Mordecai Richler, and Peter Behrens in this category, but not Brian Moore, Bharati Mukherjee, or Nino Ricci. I have tried to avoid inflating the list with writers who spent only a short time in Montreal and have in such cases limited the list to titles associated with the city. Additional documentation emailed to me at lindaleith@videotron.ca will be gratefully received and incorporated in due course into a revised bibliography.

BIBLIOGRAPHY

PRIMARY: FICTION WRITTEN IN ENGLISH[47]

Ackerman, Marianne. 2000. *Jump.* Toronto: McArthur and Company.
_____. 2005. *Matters of Hart.* McArthur and Company.
_____. 2010. *Piers' Desire.* Toronto: McArthur and Company.
Aitken, Will. 1989. *Terre Haute.* New York: Doubleday.
_____. 1993. *A Visit Home.* New York: Simon & Schuster.
_____. 2000. *Realia.* Toronto: Random House Canada.
Allen, Robert. 1980. *The Hawryliw Process.* Erin, ON: The Porcupine's Quill.
_____. 1995. *A June Night in the Late Cenozoic.* Lantzville, BC: Ooolichan.
_____. 1997. *Napoleon's Retreat.* Montreal: DC Books.
Arnopoulos, Sheila McLeod. 2000. *Jackrabbit Moon.* Vancouver: Ronsdale Press.
Ayanoglu, Byron. 2001. *Love in the Age of Confusion.* Montreal: DC Books.
Bailey, Clayton. 2003. *The Expedition.* Winnipeg: Great Plains Publications.
Basu, Arjun. 2008. *Squishy.* Montreal: DC Books.
Bath, Dana. 1998. *What Might Have Been Rain.* Montreal: Conundrum Press.
_____. 2001. *Plenty of Harm in God.* Montreal: DC Books.
_____. 2003. *Universal Recipients.* Vancouver: Arsenal Pulp Press.
Battler, Lesley. 1987. *The Polar Bear Express.* Montreal: Nuage Editions.
Behrens, Peter. 1987. *Night Driving.* Toronto: Macmillan.
_____. 2007. *The Law of Dreams.* Toronto: House of Anansi Press.
Benazon, Michael, ed. 1989. *Montréal Mon Amour.* Toronto: Deneau.
Beresford-Howe, Constance. 1946. *The Unreasoning Heart.* New York: Dodd, Mead.
_____. 1947. *Of This Day's Journey.* New York: Dodd, Mead.
_____. 1949. *The Invisible Gate.* New York: Dodd, Mead.
_____. 1955. *My Lady Greensleeves.* New York: Ballantine Books.
_____. 1973. *The Book of Eve.* Toronto: McClelland & Stewart.
_____. 1977. *A Population of One.* Toronto: McClelland & Stewart.
_____. 1981. *The Marriage Bed.* Toronto: Macmillan.
_____. 1985. *Night Studies* (1985). Toronto: Macmillan.
_____. 1988. *Prospero's Daughter.* Toronto: Macmillan.
_____. 1993. *A Serious Widow.* Toronto: McClelland & Stewart.
Bereshko, Ludmilla. 1990. *The Parcel from Chicken Street and Other Stories.* Montreal: DC Books.
Bissoondath, Neil. 1988a. *Digging Up the Mountains.* Toronto: Penguin.

_____. 1988b. *A Casual Brutality*. Toronto: Macmillan.

_____. 1991. *On the Eve of Uncertain Tomorrows*. London: Minerva.

_____. 1993. *The Innocence of Age*. Toronto: Penguin.

_____. 2003. *Doing the Heart Good*. Toronto: Cormorant.

_____. 2005. *The Unyielding Clamour of the Night*. Toronto: Cormorant.

_____. 2007. *The Worlds Within Her*. Toronto: Cormorant.

_____. 2008. *The Soul of all Great Designs*. Toronto: Cormorant.

Blair, Michael. 2001. *If Looks Could Kill*. Toronto: McClelland & Stewart.

_____. 2006. *Overexposed*. Toronto: Dundurn.

_____. 2008. *The Dells*. Toronto: Dundurn.

_____. 2009. *Depth of Field*. Toronto: Dundurn.

Blaise, Clark. 1973. *A North American Education*. Toronto: Doubleday.

_____. 1984. *Lusts*. Toronto: Penguin.

_____. 1986. *Resident Alien*. Toronto: Penguin.

_____. 1990. *Lunar Attractions*. Erin, ON: Porcupine's Quill.

_____. 2003. *Montreal Stories*. Erin, ON: Porcupine's Quill.

_____ and John Metcalf, eds. 1979. *1979 Best Canadian Stories*. Ottawa: Oberon Press.

Blomgren, Lance. 2000. *Walkups*. Montreal: Conundrum Press.

_____. 2004. *Corner Pieces*. Montreal: Conundrum Press.

Bose, Rana. 2000. *Recovering Rude*. Montreal: Véhicule Press.

_____. 2008. *The Fourth Canvas*. Toronto: TSAR Books.

Boullata, Issa J. 2007. *A Retired Gentleman and other stories*. London: Banipal Books.

Bouyoucas, Pan. 2006. *The Man Who Wanted to Drink up the Sea*. Toronto: Cormorant.

Boyarsky, Abraham. 1992. *The Number Hall*. Ottawa: Oberon Press.

Brodoff, Ami Sands. 2005. *Bloodknots*. Vancouver: Arsenal Pulp Press.

_____. 2008. *The White Space Between*. Toronto: Second Story Press.

Brooke, John. 1999. *The Voice of Aliette Nouvelle*. Winnipeg: Signature Editions.

_____. 2002. *All Pure Souls*. Winnipeg: Signature Editions.

_____. 2004. *The Last Days of Montreal*. Winnipeg: Signature Editions.

Bross, Roma Gelblum. 1988. *To Samarkand and Back*. Dunvegan, ON: Cormorant.

Brown, Andy. 2003. *I Can See You Being Invisible*. Montreal: DC Books.

_____ and Rob McLennan, eds. 2001. *You and Your Bright Ideas*. Montreal: Véhicule Press.

_____. 2006. *The Mole Chronicles*. Toronto: Insomniac Press.

Byrnes, Terry. 1980. *Wintering Over*. Dunvegan, ON Quadrant.

_____. ed. 1981. *Matinées Daily*. Dunvegan, ON: Quadrant.

Buell, John. 1959. *The Pyx*. New York: Farrar Straus & Cudahy.

_____. 1962. *Four Days*. New York: Farrar Straus & Cudahy.

_____. 1972. *The Shrewsdale Exit*. New York: Pocket Books.

_____. 1976. *Playground*. New York: Farrar Straus Giroux.

_____. 1990. *A Lot To Make Up For*. Toronto: HarperCollins.

Campbell, Wanda Blynn. 1983. *The Promise*. Vancouver: Pulp Press.

Canton, Licia. 2008. *Almond Wine and Fertility*. Montreal: Longbridge Books.

Carpenter, J.R. 2008. *Words the Dog Knows*. Montreal: Conundrum Press

Carrier, Jean-Guy. 1992. *Patriots and Traitors*. Ottawa: Oberon Press.

_____. 1993. *The End of the War*. Ottawa: Oberon Press.

Carin, Michael. 1989. *The Neutron Picasso*. Toronto: Deneau.

Carson, Anne. 1998. *Autobiography of Red: A Novel in Verse*. Toronto: Knopf.

_____. 2002. *The Beauty of the Husband*. Toronto: Knopf.

Charney, Ann. 1973, rpt. 1996. *Dobryd*. Vancouver: Douglas & McIntyre.

_____. 2001. *Rousseau's Garden*. Montreal: Véhicule Press.

_____. 2008. *Distantly Related to Freud*. Toronto: Cormorant Press.

Cohen, Leonard. 1963. *The Favorite Game*. New York: Viking.

_____. 1966. *Beautiful Losers*. New York: Viking.

Cohen, Matt and Wayne Grady, eds. 1986. *Intimate Strangers: New Fiction from Quebec*. Markham, ON: Penguin Canada.

Cowan, Judith. 1998. *More Than Life Itself*. Ottawa: Oberon Press.

_____. 2001. *Gambler's Fallacy*. Erin, ON: Porcupine's Quill.

Cox, Daniel Allen. 2008. *Shuck*. Vancouver: Arsenal Pulp Press.

_____. 2010. *Krakow Melt*. Vancouver: Arsenal Pulp Press.

Curran, Colleen. 1995. *Something Drastic*. Fredericton, NB: Goose Lane Editions.

_____. 2000. *Overnight Sensation*. Fredericton, NB: Goose Lane Editions.

_____. 2005. *Guests of Chance*. Fredericton, NB: Goose Lane Editions.

D'Alfonso, Antonio. 1995. *Fabrizio's Passion*. Toronto: Guernica Editions.

_____. 2005. *A Friday in August*. Toronto: Exile Editions, 2005.

Daymond, Douglas and Leslie Monkman, eds. 1980. *Stories of Quebec*. Ottawa: Oberon.

Decker, Ken. 1982. *Backyard Gene Pool*. Dunvegan, ON: Quadrant.

Denesiuk, Marci. 2005. *The Far Away Home*. Edmonton: NeWest Press.

Diamond, Ann. 1984 [also published as Anne McLean]. *A Nun's Diary*. Montreal: Véhicule Press.

_____. 1988. *Mona's Dance*. Kingston, ON: Quarry Press.

_____. 1989. *Snakebite*. Toronto: Cormorant.

_____. 1994. *Evil Eye*. Montreal: Véhicule Press.

_____. 2000. *Dead White Males*. Montreal: DC Books.

Di Michele, Mary. 1984. *Under My Skin*. Kingston, ON: Quarry Press.

_____. 2005. *Tenor of Love*. Toronto: HarperCollins.

Dubé, Peter. 2002. *Hovering World*. Montreal: DC Books.

_____. 2007. *At the Bottom of the Sky*. Montreal: DC Books.

_____. 2010. *Subtle Bodies*. Maple Shade, NJ: Lethe Press.

Durcan, Liam. 2004. *A Short Journey by Car*. Montreal: Véhicule Press.

_____. 2007. *Garcia's Heart*. Toronto: McClelland & Stewart.

Ferguson, Trevor [also published as John Farrow] 1977. *High Water Chants*. Toronto: Macmillan.

_____. 1985. *Onyx John*. Toronto: McClelland & Stewart.

_____. 1989. *The Kinkajou*. Toronto: McClelland & Stewart.

_____. 1993. *The True Life Adventures of Sparrow Drinkwater*. Toronto: HarperCollins.

_____. 1995. *The Fire Line*. Toronto: HarperCollins.

_____. 1996. *The Timekeeper*. Toronto: HarperCollins.

_____, as John Farrow. 1999. *City of Ice*. Toronto: HarperCollins.

_____, as John Farrow. 2001. *Ice Lake*. Toronto: HarperCollins.

Filip, Raymond. 1989. *After the Fireworks*. Montreal: Guernica Editions.

Fiorentino, Jon Paul. 2005. *Asthmatica*. Toronto: Insomniac Press.

_____. 2009. *Stripmalling*. Downsview, ON: ECW Press.

Foran, Charles. 1994. *Kitchen Music*. Dunvegan, ON: Cormorant.

_____. 1996. *Butterfly Lovers*. Toronto: HarperCollins.

Fox, Matthew. 2005. *Cities of Weather*. Toronto: Cormorant.

Fragoulis, Tess. 1997. *Stories to Hide from Your Mother*. Vancouver: Arsenal Pulp Press.

_____. 2001. *Ariadne's Dream*. Saskatoon, Sask.: Thistledown Press.

Fraser, Ray. 1973. *The Black Horse Tavern*. Montreal: Ingluvin Publications.

Frost, Corey. 2002. *My Own Devices: Airport Version*. Montreal: Conundrum Press.

_____. 2005. *The Worthwhile Flux*. Montreal: Conundrum Press.

Gagnon, Maurice. 1985. *The Inner Ring*. Don Mills, ON: Collins.

_____. 1986. *A Dark Night Offshore*. Don Mills, ON: Collins.

_____. 1987. *Doubtful Motives*. Don Mills, ON: Collins.

Gallant, Mavis. 1956. *The Other Paris*. New York: Houghton Mifflin.

_____. 1959. *Green Water, Green Sky*. New York: Houghton Mifflin.

_____. 1972. *A Fairly Good Time*. New York: Random House.

_____. 1974a. *My Heart is Broken*. Toronto: General Publishing.

_____. 1974b. *The Pegnitz Junction*. New York: Random House

_____. 1979. *From the Fifteenth District*. Toronto: Macmillan.

_____. 1981. *Home Truths*. Toronto: Macmillan.

_____. 1985. *Overhead in a Balloon*. Toronto: Macmillan.

_____. 1988. *In Transit*. New York: Viking.

_____. 1991. *The Selected Stories of Mavis Gallant*. Toronto: McClelland & Stewart.

_____. 1993. *Across the Bridge*. Toronto: McClelland & Stewart.

_____. 2009. *Going Ashore*. Toronto: McClelland & Stewart.

Gasco, Elyse. 1999. *Can You Wave Bye Bye, Baby?* Toronto: McClelland & Stewart.

Ghan, Linda. 1988. *A Gift of Sky*. Saskatoon, Sask.: Western Producer Prairie Books.

_____. 2005. *Sosi*. Winnipeg: Signature Editions.

Gillard, A.J. 2007. *Like Coming Home*. Calgary: 4th Floor Press.

_____. 2007. *Gambler's Cove*. Calgary; 4th Floor Press.

_____. 2007. *A Matter of Time*. Calgary: 4th Floor Press.

_____. 2007. *Murphy's Law*. Calgary: 4th Floor Press.

Goldbach, John. 2009. *Selected Blackouts*. Toronto: Insomniac Press.

Goldstein, Jonathan. 2001. *Lenny Bruce is Dead*. Toronto: Coach House Books.

_____. 2008. *Ladies and Gentlemen, The Bible!* Toronto: Penguin.

Graham, Gwethalyn. 1938. *Swiss Sonata*. London: Jonathan Cape.

_____. 1944. *Earth and High Heaven*. London: Jonathan Cape.

Graham, Ron. 1980. *Naughts and Crosses*. Way's Mills, Qc: Canton.

Granger, Ann Patricia. 2003. *Watching Out*. London: Headline.

Gustafson, Ralph. 1980. *The Vivid Air: Collected Stories*. Victoria, BC: Sono Nis.

Hage, Rawi. 2007. *De Niro's Game*. Toronto: House of Anansi Press.

_____. 2008. *Cockroach*. Toronto: House of Anansi Press.

Harrison, Keith. 1981. *Dead Ends*. Dunvegan, ON: Quadrant.

_____. 1985. *After Six Days*. Fredericton, NB: Goose Lane Editions.

Harvor, Elisabeth. 1988. *If Only We Could Drive This Way Forever*. Toronto: Penguin.

_____. 1996. *Let Me Be the One*. Toronto: HarperCollins.

_____. 2000. *Excessive Joy Injures the Heart*. Toronto: McClelland & Stewart.

_____. 2004. *All Times Have Been Modern*. Toronto: Viking.

Henderson, Keith. 1987. *The Restoration: The Referendum Years*. Montreal: DC Books.

_____. 1990. *The Beekeeper*. Montreal: DC Books.

_____. 2005. *The Pagan Nuptials of Julia, and other stories*. Montreal: DC Books.

Henighan, Stephen. 1990. *Other Americas*. Toronto: Simon and Pierre Publishing.

_____. 1992. *Nights in the Yungas*. Calgary: 4th Floor Press.

Hoefle, Harold. 2008. *The Mountain Clinic*. Ottawa: Oberon Press.

Holden, Hélène. 1986. *After the Fact*. Ottawa: Oberon Press.

_____. 1988. *Snow*. Ottawa: Oberon Press.

Holtz, Nairne. 2007. *The Skin Beneath*. Toronto: Insomniac Press.

_____. 2009. *This One's Going to Last Forever*. Toronto: Insomniac Press.

Homel, David. 1988. *Electrical Storms*. Toronto: Random House.

_____. 1992. *Rat Palms*. Toronto: HarperCollins.

_____. 1995. *Sonya and Jack*. Toronto: HarperCollins.

_____. 1999. *Get on Top*. Toronto: Stoddart.

_____. 2003. *The Speaking Cure*. Vancouver: Douglas & McIntyre.

_____. 2010. *Midway*. Toronto: Cormorant.

Hood, Andrew. 2008. *Pardon our Monsters*. Montreal: Véhicule Press.

Hood, Hugh. 1962. *Flying a Red Kite*. Toronto: Ryerson Press.

_____. 1964. *White Figure, White Ground*. Toronto: Ryerson Press.

_____. 1967a. *Around the Mountain: Scenes from Montreal Life*. Toronto: Peter Martin.

_____. 1967b. *The Camera Always Lies*. New York: Harcourt Brace.

_____. 1970. *A Game of Touch*. Don Mills, ON: Longman.

_____. 1971. *The Fruit Man, The Meat Man & The Manager*. Ottawa: Oberon Press.

_____. 1972. *You Can't Get There From Here*. Ottawa: Oberon Press.

_____. 1975. *The Swing in the Garden*. Ottawa: Oberon Press.

_____. 1976. *Dark Glasses*. Ottawa: Oberon Press.

_____. 1977. *A New Athens*. Ottawa: Oberon Press.

_____.1978. *Selected Stories*. Ottawa: Oberon Press.

_____. 1979. *Reservoir Ravine*. Downsview, ON: ECW Press.

_____. 1980. *None Genuine Without This Signature*. Downsview, ON: ECW Press.

_____. 1982. *Black and White Keys*. Downsview, ON ECW Press.

_____. 1984. *The Scenic Art*. Toronto: Stoddart.

_____. 1985. *August Nights*. Toronto: Stoddart.

_____. 1986. *The Motor Boys in Ottawa*. Toronto: Stoddard.

_____. 1987. *Five New Facts about Giorgione*. Windsor, ON: Black Moss Press.

_____. 1988. *Tony's Book*. Toronto: Stoddard.

_____. 1989. *A Short Walk in the Rain*. Erin, ON: Porcupine's Quill.

_____.1990. *Property & Value*. Toronto: House of Anansi Press.

_____.1991. *The Isolation Booth*. Erin, ON: Porcupine's Quill.

_____. 1992. *You'll Catch Your Death*. Erin, ON: Porcupine's Quill.

_____.1993. *Be Sure to Close Your Eyes*. Toronto: House of Anansi Press

_____. 1995. *Dead Men's Watches*. Toronto: House of Anansi Press

_____.1997. *Great Realizations*. Toronto: House of Anansi Press

_____. 2001. *Near Water*. Erin, ON: Porcupine's Quill.

_____. 2003. *After All*. Erin, ON: Porcupine's Quill.

_____ and Peter O'Brien, eds. 1984. *Fatal Recurrences: New Fiction in English from Montreal*. Montreal: Véhicule.

Howe, Valmai. 1988. *The Dreams of Zoo Animals*. Montreal: Nuage Editions.

_____. 1992. *The Loneliness of Angels*. Montreal: Nuage Editions.

Iannuzzi, D.C. 2008. *City of Sinners*. Montreal: Longbridge Books.

Jensen, Catholyn K. 1990. *Birds of a Feather*. Montreal: Véhicule Press.

Kalynchuk, Valerie Joy. 2001. *All Day Breakfast*. Montreal: Conundrum Press.

_____. 2006. *Beauty is a Liar*. Montreal: Conundrum Press.

Karafilly, Irena Friedman. 1990. *Night Cries*. Ottawa: Oberon Press.

Kaslik, Ibi. 2004. *Skinny*. Toronto: HarperCollins.

_____. 2008. *The Angel Riots*. Toronto: Penguin.

Kidd, Catherine. 2006. *bipolar bear*. Montreal: Conundrum Press.

_____. 2007. *Missing the Ark*. Montreal: Conundrum Press.

_____ and Jack Beetz. 2002. *Sea Peach*. Montreal: Conundrum Press.

Keightley, Liane. 2008. *Seven Openings of the Head*. Montreal: Conundrum.

Keith, Julie. 1996. *The Jaguar Temple and other stories*. Montreal: Nuage Editions.

_____. 2000. *The Devil Out There: A Novella and Stories*. Toronto: Knopf.

Kevan, Martin. 1984. *Racing Tides*. Toronto: Stoddart.

King, Richard. 2001. *That Sleep of Death*. Toronto: Dundurn Press.

Kingsbury, Donald. 1982. *Courtship Rite*. New York: Simon.

_____. 1986. *The Moon Goddess and the Son*. New York: Simon.

Klein, A.M. 1982. *A.M. Klein, Short Stories*. Ed. M.W. Steinberg. Toronto: University of Toronto Press.

_____. 1951. *The Second Scroll*. New York: Knopf.

Kramer, Greg. 2004. *Wally*. Toronto: Cormorant Books.

Lalumière, Claude, ed. 2004. *Island Dreams: Montreal Writers of the Fantastic*. Montreal: Véhicule Press.

_____ and Rupert Bottenberg (illus.). 2009. *Objects of Worship*. ChiZine Publications.

Landori, Robert. 2004. *Fatal Greed*. Montreal: Studio 9.

Lavery, John. 2000. *Very Good Butter*. Downsview, ON: ECW Press.

_____. 2004. *You, Kwaznievski, You Piss Me Off*. Downsview, ON: ECW Press.

_____. 2010. *Sandra Beck*. Toronto: House of Anansi Press.

Lawrence, P. Scott. 1984. *Around the Mulberry Tree*. Toronto: Exile Editions.

_____. ed. 1987. *Souvenirs: New English Fiction from Quebec*. Dunvegan, ON: Cormorant.

Leith, Linda, Guest ed. 1988. *Canadian Fiction Magazine*, No. 63, special issue on New English Fiction from Quebec; reprinted 1989 as *Telling Differences: New English Fiction from Quebec*. Montreal: Véhicule Press.

_____. 1993. *Birds of Passage*. Montreal: Nuage Editions.

_____. 1995. *The Tragedy Queen*. Montreal: Nuage Editions.

_____. 2007. *The Desert Lake*. Winnipeg: Signature Editions.

Loewen, Grant. 1992. *Brick, Looking Up*. Montreal: DC Books.

Luxton, Steve, ed. 1981. *Saturday Night at the Forum*. Dunvegan, ON: Quadrant.

MacIntyre, Wendy. 1992. *Mairi*. Lantzville, B.C.: Oolichan Books.

_____. 2003. *The Applecross Spell*. Montreal: XYZ Publishing.

MacLennan, Hugh. 1941. *Barometer Rising: A Novel of Halifax in War Time*. New York: Duell, Sloan and Pearce.

_____. 1945. *Two Solitudes*. New York: Duell, Sloan and Pearce.

_____. 1959. *The Watch That Ends the Night*. Toronto: Macmillan.

_____. 1948. *The Precipice*. Toronto: Macmillan.

_____. 1951. *Each Man's Son*. Toronto: Macmillan.

_____. 1967. *Return of the Sphinx*. Toronto: Macmillan.

_____. 1980. *Voices in Time*. Toronto: Macmillan.

Majzels, Robert. 1992. *Hellmann's Scrapbook*. Dunvegan, Ont.: Cormorant Books.

_____. 1997. *City of Forgetting*. Toronto: Mercury Press.

_____. 2004. *Apikoros Sleuth*. Toronto: Mercury Press.

Manicom, David. 1997. *Ice in Dark Water*. Montreal: Véhicule Press.

_____. 2005. *The School at Chartres*. Calgary: 4th Floor Press.

_____. 2008. *Anna's Shadow*. Montreal: Véhicule Press.

Manners, Steven. 2002. *Wound Ballistics*. Toronto: Gutter Press.

Marshall, Joyce. 1946. *Presently Tomorrow*. Boston: Little, Brown.

_____. 1957. *Lovers and Strangers*. Boston: Little, Brown.

Martel, Yann. 1993. *The Facts Behind the Helsinki Roccamatios*. Toronto: Random House.

_____. 1996. *Self*. Toronto: Knopf.

_____. 2001. *Life of Pi*. Toronto: Knopf.

_____. 2010. *Beatrice and Virgil*. Toronto: Knopf.

McAdam, Colin. 2004. *Some Great Thing*. Vancouver: Raincoast.

_____. 2009. *Fall*. Toronto: Penguin.

McArthur, Nick. 2009. *Short Accounts of Tragic Occurrences*. Montreal: DC Books.

McBain, Daniel. 1991. *Art Roebuck comes to Born with a Tooth*. Montreal: DC Books.

McDevitt, Neale. 2002. *One Day Even Trevi Will Crumble*. Toronto: Exile Editions.

McGillis, Ian. 2002. *A Tourist's Guide To Glengarry*. Erin, ON: Porcupine's Quill.

McGimpsey, David. 2004. *Certifiable*. Toronto: Insomniac Press.

McGregor, Stephen. 2008. *Two Trails Narrow*. Penticton, B.C.: Theytus Books.

Merrick, Maya. 2005. *Sextant*. Calgary: 4th Floor Press.

———. 2007. *The Hole Show*. Montreal: Conundrum Press.

Metcalf, John. 1970. *The Lady Who Sold Furniture*. Toronto: Clarke Irwin.

———. 1972. *Going Down Slow*. Toronto: McClelland & Stewart.

———. 1975. *The Teeth of My Father*. Ottawa: Oberon Press.

———. 1980. *General Ludd*. Downsview, ON: ECW Press.

Mirolla, Michael. 1991. *The Formal Logic of Emotion*. Montreal: Nuage Editions.

———. 2010. *The Facility*. Falmouth, Mass: Leapfrog Press.

Montrose, David (pen name of Charles Ross Graham). 1951. *The Crime on Côte des Neiges*, rpt. Montreal: Véhicule Press, 2010.

———. 1952. *Murder over Dorval*, rpt Montreal: Véhicule Press, 2010.

Moore, Brian. 1956. *The Lonely Passion of Judith Hearne*. Boston: Back Bay Books.

———. 1957. *The Feast of Lupercal*. Boston: Little Brown.

———. 1960. *The Luck of Ginger Coffey*. New York: Little Brown.

———. 1971. *The Revolution Script*. Toronto: McClelland & Stewart.

Moore, Jeffrey. 1999. *Prisoner in a Red-Rose Chain*. Saskatoon, SK: Thistledown Press.

———. 2004. *The Memory Artists*. Toronto: Penguin.

———. 2010. *The Extinction Club*. Toronto: Penguin.

Morrison, Claudia. 1992. *From the Foot of the Mountain*. Dunvegan, ON: Cormorant.

———. *I Should Know and Other Stories*. Pointe-Claire, QC: Morgaine House.

Moser, Elise. 2009. *Because I Have Loved and Hidden It*. Toronto: Cormorant.

Mukherjee, Bharati. 1985. *Darkness*. Toronto: Penguin Books.

———. 1971. *The Tiger's Daughter*. New York: Houghton Mifflin.

———. 1975. *Wife*. New York: Houghton Mifflin.

Naraghi, Akhtar. 1999. *The Big Green House*. Montreal: Cedah.

———. 1999. *Blue Curtains*. Montreal: Cedah.

———. 2004. *With Mara That Summer*. Montreal: Cedah.

Nasrallah, Dimitri. 2004. *Blackbodying*. Montreal: DC Books.

Nawaz, Saleema. 2008. *Mother Superior*. Calgary: Freehand Books.

Nemiroff, Daniel. 2007. *Nasty, Short and Brutal*. Toronto: Exile Editions.

Nugent, Jacqueline. 1990. *The Glass Treehouse*. Toronto: Viking.

O'Neill, Heather. 2006. *Lullabies for Little Criminals*. Toronto: HarperCollins.

Packer, Miriam. 1993. *Take Me to Coney Island*. Montreal: Guernica.

———. 2000. *Us Fools Believing*. Toronto: Guernica.

———. 2003. *Song for my Father*. Toronto: Guernica.

Paterson, Mark. 2003. *Other People's Showers*. Toronto: Exile Editions.

———. 2007. *A Finely Tuned Apathy Machine*. Toronto: Exile Editions.

Peng, Jia-Lin. 1990. *Wild Cat*. Dunvegan, ON: Cormorant.

Penny, Louise. 2005. *Still Life*. London: Hodder Headline.

_____. 2007a. *Dead Cold*. London. Hodder Headline.

_____. 2007b. *The Cruelest Month*. London: Hodder Headline.

_____. 2008. *The Murder Stone*. London: Hodder Headline.

_____. 2009. *The Brutal Telling*. London: Hodder Headline.

Phillips, Edward. 1986. *Buried on Sunday*. Toronto: McClelland & Stewart.

_____. 1988. *Hope Springs Eternal*. Toronto: McClelland & Stewart.

_____. 1982. *Sunday's Child*. Toronto: McClelland & Stewart.

_____. 1984. *Where There's a Will*. Toronto: McClelland & Stewart, Rpt. as Death is Relative. New York: Avon, 1985.

_____. 1990. *Sunday Best*. Toronto: Seal.

_____. 1992. *The Landlady's Niece*. Toronto: McClelland Bantam.

_____. 1996. *The Mice Will Play*. Toronto: Riverbank.

_____. 1998. *Working on Sunday*. Toronto: Riverbank.

_____. 2004. *A Voyage On Sunday*. Toronto: Cormorant.

_____. 2007. *Queen's Court*. Toronto: Riverbank.

Radu, Kenneth. 1987. *The Cost of Living*. Dorion, QC: The Muses' Company/ La Compagnie des Muses.

_____. 1989. *Distant Relations*. Ottawa: Oberon.

_____. 1992. *Home Fires*. Montreal: Véhicule Press.

_____. 1990. *A Private Performance*. Montreal: Véhicule Press.

_____. 1994. *Snow Over Judea*. Montreal: Véhicule Press.

_____. 1999. *Strange & Familiar Places*. Montreal: Véhicule Press.

_____. 2001. *Flesh and Blood*. Toronto: HarperCollins.

_____. 2004. *The Purest of Human Pleasures*. Toronto: Penguin.

_____. 2010. *Sex in Russia: New and Selected Stories*. Montreal: DC Books.

Rastelli, Louis. 2007. *A Fine Ending*. Toronto: Insomniac Press.

Rau Badami, Anita. 1999. *Tamarind Mem*. Chapel Hill, NC: Algonquin Books.

_____. 1997. *The Hero's Walk*. Toronto: Knopf Canada.

_____. 2006. *Can You Hear the Nightbird Call?* Toronto: Knopf Canada.

Ravel, Edeet (also published as Edeet Ross). 1994. *Lovers: A Midrash*. Montreal: Nuage Editions.

_____. 2003. *Ten Thousand Lovers*. London: Review Books.

_____. 2005. *A Wall of Light*. Toronto: Random House.

_____. 2004. *Look For Me*. Toronto: Random House.

Ravvin, Norman. 2003. *Lola by Night*. Toronto: Paper Plates Press.

Ricci, Nino. 1990. *Lives of the Saints*. Dunvegan, ON: Cormorant.

Richler, Mordecai. 1954. *The Acrobats*. London: André Deutsch.

_____. 1955. *Son of a Smaller Hero*. London: André Deutsch.

_____. 1957. *A Choice of Enemies*. London: André Deutsch.

_____. 1959. *The Apprenticeship of Duddy Kravitz*. London: André Deutsch.

_____. 1963. *The Incomparable Atuk*. London: André Deutsch.

_____. 1968. *Cocksure*. London: Weidenfeld & Nicholson.

_____. 1969. *The Street*. Toronto: McClelland & Stewart.

_____. 1971. *St. Urbain's Horseman*. Toronto: McClelland & Stewart.

_____. 1980. *Joshua Then and Now*. Toronto: McClelland & Stewart.

_____. 1989. *Solomon Gursky Was Here*. Toronto: Viking.

_____. 1997. *Barney's Version*. Toronto: Knopf.

Rigelhof, T.F. 1981. "Hans Denck, Cobbler." *A Beast with Two Backs: Two Novels*. Ottawa: Oberon Press, 49-95.

_____. 1983. *The Education of J.J. Pass*. Ottawa: Oberon Press.

_____. 1993. *Je t'aime, Cowboy*. Ottawa, ON: Oberon Press.

_____. 1992. *Badass on a Softail*. Fredericton, NB: Goose Lane Editions.

Roig, Denise. 1995. *A Quiet Night and a Perfect End*. Montreal: Nuage Editions.

_____. 2005. *Any Day Now*. Winnipeg: Signature Editions.

Rothman, Claire (also published as Claire Holden Rothman.) 1990. *Salad Days*. Ottawa: Oberon Press.

_____. 1999. *Black Tulips*. Ottawa: Oberon Press.

_____. 2008. As Claire Holden Rothman. *The Heart Specialist*. Toronto: Cormorant.

Samuel, Julian. *Passage to Lahore*. Stratford, ON: Mercury.

Sarah, Robyn. 1992. *A Nice Gazebo*. Montreal: Véhicule Press.

Scott, Gail. 1982. *Spare Parts*. Stratford, ON: Mercury.

_____. 1987. *Heroine*. Toronto: Coach House Books.

_____. 1993. *Main Brides*. Toronto: Coach House Books.

_____. 1999. *My Paris*. Stratford, ON: Mercury.

_____. 2010. *The Obituary*. Toronto, ON: Coach House Books.

Siblin, Eric. 2009. *The Cello Suites*. Toronto: House of Anansi Press.

Singh, Jaspreet. 2004. *Seventeen Tomatoes: Tales from Kashmir*. Montreal: Véhicule Press.

_____. 2008. *Chef*. Montreal: Véhicule Press.

Skibsrud, Johanna. 2009. *The Sentimentalists*. Kentville, NS: Gaspereau Press.

Smith, Neil. 2007. *Bang Crunch*. Toronto: Knopf.

Smith, Ray. 1969. *Cape Breton is the Thought Control Centre of Canada*. Toronto: House of Anansi Press.

_____. 1974. *Lord Nelson's Tavern*. Toronto: McClelland & Stewart.

_____. 1986. *Century*. Toronto: Stoddart.

_____. 1999. *The Man Who Loved Jane Austen*. Erin, ON: Porcupine's Quill.

Soderstrom, Mary. 1976. *The Descent of Andrew McPherson*. Toronto: McGraw Hill-Ryerson Press.

———. 1982. *Maybe Tomorrow I'll Have a Good Time*. New York: Human Sciences Press.

———. 1995. *Endangered Species*. Ottawa: Oberon Press.

———. 1997. *Finding the Enemy*. Ottawa: Oberon Press.

———. 2000. *The Truth Is*. Ottawa: Oberon Press.

———. 2004. *After Surfing Ocean Beach*. Toronto: Dundurn.

———. 2008. *The Violets of Usambara*. Toronto: Cormorant Books.

Sorfleet, Robert, ed. 1980. Quebec Fiction: The English Fact [special issue] *Journal of Canadian Fiction* 30.

Sparling, Sharon. 1985. *The Glass Mountain*. Toronto: Doubleday.

———. 1991. *The Nest Egg*. Toronto: Macmillan.

Spencer, Elizabeth. 1959. *The Light in the Piazza*. New York: McGraw-Hill.

———. 1981. *The Stories of Elizabeth Spencer*. New York: Doubleday.1981

———. 1988. *Jack and Diamonds and Other Stories*. New York: Viking.

———. 1984. *The Salt Line*. New York: Doubleday.

———. 1981. *Marilee*. Jackson: University of Mississippi Press.

Steinberg, Donna. 1983. *I Lost it All in Montreal*. New York: Avon.

———. 1988. *Fat Chance*. Montreal: Eden.

Stone, Anne. 1998. *jacks: a gothic gospel*. Montreal: DC Books.

Syjuco, Miguel. 2010. *Ilustrado*. Toronto: Penguin Books.

Symons, Scott. 1967. *Place d'Armes*. Toronto: McClelland & Stewart.

Szanto, George. 1982. *Not Working*. Toronto: Macmillan.

———. 1978. *Sixteen Ways to Skin a Cat*. Vancouver: Intermedia Press.

———. 1995. *Friends and Marriages*. Montreal: Véhicule Press:

———. 2000. *The Underside of Stones*. Toronto: McClelland & Stewart.

———. 2004. *Second Sight*. Montreal: XYZ Publishing.

———. 2005. *The Condesa of M*. Montreal: XYZ Publishing.

———, with Per Brask. 1989. *Duets*. Saskatoon: Coteau Books.

Tausch, Julia. 2003. *Another Book About Another Broken Heart*. Montreal: Conundrum Press.

Ternar, Yeshim. 1996. *True Romance with a Sailor*. Montreal: Véhicule Press.

———. 1998. *Rembrandt's Model*. Montreal: Véhicule Press.

———. 1989. *Lighter in Spirit*. Stratford, ON: Williams Wallace.

Thien, Madeleine. 2006. *Certainty*. Toronto: McClelland & Stewart.

Thomas, H. Nigel. 1993. *Spirits in the Dark*. Toronto: House of Anansi Press.

———. 1994. *How Loud Can the Village Cock Crow?* St. Laurent, QC: Afo.

———. 2001. *Behind the Face of Winter*. Toronto: TSAR.

———. 2007. *Return to Arcadia*. Toronto: TSAR.

Vlassie, Katherine. 1987. *Letters to Byzantium*. Dunvegan, ON: Cormorant.

Von Westrenen, Pieter Anton. 1985. *The Vortical Man*. Montreal and Paris: Editions Two Cities.

Webb, Paddy. 1984. *Rough Passage*. Dunvegan, ON: Quadrant.

Weintraub, William. 1961. *Don't Rock the Boat*. Boston: Little, Brown.

_____. 1979. *The Underdogs*. Toronto: McClelland & Stewart.

Wexler, Jerry. 1984. *The Bequest and Other Stories*. Montreal: Véhicule Press.

Whittall, Zoe. 2007. *Bottle Rocket Hearts*. Toronto: Cormorant.

Winter, Kathleen. 2010. *Annabel*. Toronto: House of Anansi Press.

Yanofsky, Joel. 1997. *Jacob's Ladder*. Erin, ON: Porcupine's Quill.

Zorn, Alice. 2008. *Ruins and Relics*. Edmonton: NeWest Press.

SECONDARY SOURCES

Abley, Mark. 2003. *Spoken Here: Travels Among Threatened Languages.* Toronto: Random House.

_____. 2008. *The Prodigal Tongue: Dispatches from the Future of English.* New York: Houghton Mifflin.

Aquin, Hubert. 1965. *Prochain épisode.* Montréal: Cercle du livre de France.

Arnopoulos, Sheila McLeod and Dominique Clift. 1980. *The English Fact in Quebec.* Montreal: McGill-Queens University Press.

Association of English-Language Publishers of Quebec and Quebec Writers' Federation. 2005. Quebec English-language Writers and Publishers Research Project. N.p.

Atwood, Margaret. 1972. *Survival: A Thematic Guide to Canadian Literature.* Toronto: House of Anansi Press.

_____. 1972. *Surfacing.* Toronto: McClelland & Stewart.

_____ and Robert Weaver, eds. 1986. *The Oxford Book of Canadian Short Stories in English.* Toronto: Oxford University Press.

Bérubé, Nicholas. 2010. "Les anglos et les immigrants sont ignorés". *La Presse* (Montréal), 6 juillet 2010.

Biron, Michel, François Dumont, et Élisabeth Nardout-Lafarge. 2007. *Histoire de la littérature québécoise.* Montréal: Boréal.

Bissonnette, Lise. 1996. "Dans une librairie." *Le Devoir* (Montréal), 12 février 1996.

Blais, Marie-Claire. 1959. *La belle bête.* Montréal: Pierre Tisseyre.

Bourassa, André G. 1977. *Surréalisme et littérature québécoise.* Montréal: L'Étincelle.

Bourhis, R.Y., ed. 2008. *The Vitality of the English-Speaking Communities of Quebec: From Community Decline to Revival.* Montréal: CEETUM, Université de Montréal.

Burnard, Bonnie. 1989. Review of *Telling Differences: New English Fiction from Quebec. The Globe and Mail* (Toronto), May 6, 1989.

Cameron, Elspeth. 1981. *Hugh MacLennan: A Writer's Life.* Toronto: University of Toronto Press.

Camlot, Jason. 2007. "Introduction: Anglo-Québec Poetry, (b. 1976-). *Language Acts: Anglo-Quebec Poetry, 1976 to the 21st Century,* eds. Jason Camlot and Todd Swift. Montreal: Véhicule Press, 13-35.

_____ and Todd Swift, eds. 2007. *Language Acts: Anglo-Quebec Poetry, 1976 to the 21st Century.* Montreal: Véhicule Press.

Charney, Ann. 1995. *Defiance in Their Eyes: True Stories from the Margins.* Montreal: Véhicule Press.

Coleman, Patrick. 1993. *The Limits of Sympathy: Gabrielle Roy's The Tin Flute*. Downsview, ON: ECW Press.

Creighton, Donald. 1970. *Canada's First Century 1867-1967*. Toronto: Macmillan.

Deane, Seamus. 1986. *A Short History of Irish Literature*. London: Hutchinson.

Deleuze, Gilles et Félix Guattari. 1975. *Kafka: Pour une littérature mineure*. Paris: Éditions du Minuit; *Kafka: Toward a Minor Literature*, trans. Dana Polan. 1986. Minneapolis: University of Minnesota Press.

Demchinsky, Bryan and Elaine Kalman Naves. 2000. *Storied Streets: Montreal in the Literary Imagination*. Toronto: Macfarlane Walter & Ross.

Entzminger, Betina. 1994. "An Interview with Elizabeth Spencer." *The Mississippi Quarterly*, Vol. 47.

Fennario, David. 1972. *Without a Parachute*. Privately printed.

_____. 1984. *Blue Mondays*. Verdun, QC: Black Rock Creations.

Floch, William and Joanne Pocock. 2008. "The Socio-Economic Status of English-Speaking Quebecers: Those Who Left and Those Who Stayed," in R.Y. Bourhis, ed. 2008. *The Vitality of the English-Speaking Communities of Quebec: From Community Decline to Revival*. Montréal: CEETUM, Université de Montréal, 35-62.

Foster, John Wilson. 1987. *Fictions of the Irish Literary Revival: A Changeling Art*. Syracuse, NY: Syracuse University Press, Gill and Macmillan.

Foster, R.F. 1997. *W.B. Yeats: The Apprentice Mage*, vol. 1. London: Oxford University Press.

Fraser, Blair. 1967. *The Search for Identity: Canada 1945-1967*. NY and Toronto: Doubleday.

Fraser, Graham. 2006. *Sorry, I Don't Speak French: Confronting the Canadian Crisis that Won't Go Away*. Toronto: McClelland & Stewart.

Freed, Josh and Jon Kalina. 1983. *The Anglo Guide to Survival in Quebec*. Montreal: Eden Press.

Gadpaille, Michelle. 1989. *The Canadian Short Story*. New York: Oxford University Press.

Godbout, Jacques. 1967. *Salut Galarneau!* Paris: Éditions du Seuil.

Gollner, Adam Leith. 2008. *The Fruit Hunters*. New York: Charles Scribner & Sons.

Grant, George. 1965. *Lament for a Nation: The Defeat of Canadian Nationalism*. Toronto: McClelland & Stewart.

Grescoe, Taras. 2000. *Sacré Blues: An Unsentimental Journey Through Quebec*. Toronto: Macfarlane Walter & Ross.

_____. 2003. *The End of Elsewhere: Travels Among the Tourists*. Toronto: Macfarlane Walter & Ross.

_____. 2006. *The Devil's Picnic*. Toronto: HarperCollins.

_____. 2008. *Bottomfeeder*. Toronto: HarperCollins.

Guèvremont, Germaine. 1945. *Le Survenant*. Montréal: Éditions Beauchemin.

_____. 1947. *Marie-Didace*. Montréal : Éditions Beauchemin.

Hancock, Geoff. 1978. "Interview with Mavis Gallant." *Canadian Fiction Magazine*. 28: 18-67.

Harel, Simon. 2007/2008. "Les loyautés conflictuelles de la littérature québécoise." *Québec Studies*, 44, 41-53.

Homel, David. "La littérature du voisin: le festival bleu." *La Presse*, 2 avril 2000. B3.

Jacobs, Jane. 1980. *The Question of Separatism: Quebec and the Struggle over Sovereignty*. New York: Vintage Books.

Jedwab, Jack. 2008. "How Shall We Define Thee? Determining who is an English-Speaking Quebecer and Assessing its Demographic Vitality." In R.Y. Bourhis, ed. 2008. *The Vitality of the English-Speaking Communities of Quebec: From Community Decline to Revival*. Montréal: CEETUM, Université de Montréal, 1-18.

King, Richard. 2009. "Remembrance of QSPELL Past." Poetry-Quebec. http://www.poetry-quebec.com/pq/history/article_65.shtml [website].

Layton, Irving. *Engagements*. Toronto: McClelland & Stewart, 1972.

_____. 1948. *Now is the Place*. Montreal: First Statement.

_____. 1961. *The Swinging Flesh*. Toronto: McClelland & Stewart.

_____ (with David O'Rourke). 1985. *Waiting for the Messiah: A Memoir*. Toronto: McClelland & Stewart.

Lecker, Robert. 2006. *Dr Delicious: Memoirs of a Life in CanLit*. Montreal: Véhicule Press.

Leclerc, Catherine. 2007/2008. "Détournements amoureux: lire en anglais au Québec." *Québec Studies*, 44, 71-82.

Leith, Linda. 1987. Tapes of unpublished interviews, Concordia University archives.

_____. 1989/1990. "English Quebec Fiction in the 1980s: A Case Study in Marginality." *Québec Studies*, 9, 95-110, rpt. *Studies in Canadian Literature*, 15, 1, 1-20.

_____. 1990. *Introducing Hugh MacLennan's Two Solitudes*. Downsview, ON: ECW Press.

_____. 1998/1999. "Commentaires." *Québec Studies* 16, 15-16.

_____, trans. 2000. *Travels with an Umbrella: An Irish Journey*. Winnipeg: Signature Editions.

_____. 2007/2008. "Blue Metropolis and the Evolution of Quebec Literature." *Québec Studies*, 44, 53-64.

_____. 2008. *Marrying Hungary*. Winnipeg: Signature Editions.

Lemelin, Roger. 1944. *Au pied de la pente douce*. Montréal: Éditions de l'Arbre.

_____. 1948. *Les Plouffe*. Québec : Bélisle éditeur.

Lennox, John and Michele Lacombe. 1988. *Dear Bill: The Correspondence of William Arthur Deacon*. Toronto: University of Toronto Press.

Letelier-Ruz, Elias. 2010. "A Short History of FEWQ." Poetry Quebec 5. http://www.poetryquebec.com [website].

Levine, Marc V. 1990. *The Reconquest of Montreal: Language Policy and Social Change in a Bilingual City*. Philadelphia: Temple University Press.

Majzels, Robert. 2007/2008. "Despair as Oppositional Practice: Writing the Minority Within Quebec's English Minority." *Québec Studies*, 44, 65-70.

Manguel, Alberto. 2000. "The Power of Babel." *The Globe and Mail* (Toronto), 15 April 2000, A 32.

Marcotte, Gilles. 1998/1999. "Neil Bissoondath disait…." *Québec Studies*, 26, 6-11.

McPherson, Don. 2010. "Québécois are maîtres — Quebecers are invités." *The Gazette* (Montreal), August 5, 201

Metcalf, John. 1988. *What Is A Canadian Literature?* Guelph, ON: Red Kite Press.

Moyes, Lianne. 2007/2008. "Conflict in Contiguity: An Update." *Québec Studies*, 44, 1-20.

_____ et Gillian Lane-Mercier, éds. 2007/2008. Textes, territoires, traduction: (dé)localisations/dislocations de la littérature anglo-québécoise. *Québec Studies*, 44, 1-20.

Naves, Elaine Kalman. 1993. *The Writers of Montreal*. Montreal: Véhicule Press.

_____. 1996. *Journey to Vaja: Reconstructing the World of a Hungarian-Jewish Family*. Montreal and Kingston: McGill Queen's University Press.

_____. 1998. *Putting Down Roots: Montreal Immigrant Writers*. Montreal: Véhicule Press.

_____. 2003. *Shoshanna's Story*. Toronto: McClelland & Stewart.

_____. 2007. *Robert Weaver: Godfather of Canadian Literature*. Montreal: Véhicule Press.

Nischik, Reinhard M., ed. 2007. *The Canadian Short Story: Interpretations*. Rochester, NY: Camden House.

Norris, Ken, ed. 1993. *Vehicule Days: An Unorthodox History of Montreal's Vehicule Poets*. Montreal: Nuage Editions.

Paskal, Cleo. 2010. *Global Warring*. Toronto: Key Porter.

Philpot, Robin. 2005. *Le Référendum volé*. Montréal: Les Intouchables.

Pozier, Bernard. 2005. "Montréal et puis." *L'Unique*, décembre 2005, 10.

Potts, Robert. 2003. "Light in the Wilderness" (profile of Margaret Atwood). *The Guardian* (London). Saturday 26 April 2003.

Prosperi, P. 1995. *The Dynamics of Ethno-Linguistic Mobilisation in Canada: A Case Study of Alliance Quebec*. Ottawa: University of Ottawa Press.

Québec, Gouvernement du. 1995. Projet de la loi sur la souveraineté du Québec. http://www.ncf.ca/ip/newspaper/ledroit/services/loi.pq [website].

Radice, Martha. 2000. "Feeling comfortable?" *Les Anglo-Montréalais et leur ville*. Sainte-Foy: Les Presses de l'Université Laval. Published in English by the same press as "Feeling Comfortable?" *The Urban Experience of Anglo-Montrealers*.

Reid, Gregory. https://dictio.flsh.usherbrooke.ca/thematique/ar78.html [website].

Richler, Mordecai. 1992. *Oh Canada! Oh Quebec! Requiem for a Divided Country*. New York: Alfred A. Knopf.

Rigelhof, T.F. 2000. *This Is Our Writing*. Erin, ON: Porcupine's Quill.

_____. 2010. *Hooked on Canadian Books: The Good, the Better and the Best Canadian Novels Since 1984*. Toronto: Cormorant.

Roy, Gabrielle. 1945. *Bonheur d'occasion*. 2 vols. Montréal: Société des Éditions Pascal.

Rudin, Ronald. 1985. *The Forgotten Quebecers: A History of English-Speaking Quebec 1759-1980*. Montreal: IQRC.

Rybczynski, Witold. 1986. *Home: A Short History of an Idea*. New York: Viking.

Salée, Daniel. 1977. "Quebec Sovereignty and the Challenge of Linguistic and Ethnocultural Minorities: Identity, Difference and the Politics of Ressentiment." *Québec Studies*, 24, 6-23.

Saul, John Ralston. 1997. *Reflections of a Siamese Twin: Canada at the Beginning of the Twenty-First Century*. Toronto: Penguin.

Schubert, Lori. 2010. "Calling North America…." Letter to the editor, *The New York Times Book Review*, Sunday, July 27, 2010. Rpt *Montreal Review of Books*, Spring 2010, 10.

Shek, Ben-Zion. 1977. *Social Realism in the French-Canadian Novel*. Montreal: Harvest House.

Simon, Sherry. 2006. *Translating Montreal: Episodes in the Life of a Divided City*. Montreal, Kingston: McGill-Queen's University Press.

Smith, Donald. 1986. *Voices of Deliverance: Interviews with Quebec and Acadian Writers*. Trans. Larry Shouldice. Toronto: Anansi.

Solway, David. 2002. "Double Exile and Montreal English-Language Poetry." In Camlot and Swift, eds. 2007, *Language Acts: Anglo-Quebec Poetry, 1976 to the 21st Century*, 80-86.

_____. 2009. http://www.notesandqueries.ca/found-in-translation [website].

Statistics Canada. 1971, 1981, 1991, 2001, 2006. Census of Canada. Public Use Microdata File.

Stevenson, Garth. 1999. *Community Besieged: The Anglophone Minority and the Politics of Quebec*. Montreal: McGill-Queen's University Press.

Stewart, Robert. 1989. Review of Telling Differences: New English Fiction from Quebec. *The Gazette* (Montreal). April 1, 1989.

Struthers, J.R. (Tim), ed. 1985. *The Montreal Story Tellers: Memoirs, Photographs, Critical Essays*. Montreal: Véhicule Press.

Suvin, Darko. 1979. *Metamorphoses of Science Fiction: On the Poetics and History of a Literary Genre*. New Haven: Yale University Press.

Taylor, Charles (1935-1997). 1977. *Six Journeys: A Canadian Pattern*. Toronto: House of Anansi Press.

Taylor, Charles (b. 1931). 1993. *Reconciling the Solitudes*, ed Guy Laforest. Montreal: McGill-Queen's University Press.

Théoret, France and Jean Stafford. 1967. "À propos de Roland Giguère." *La Barre du jour*, 11-12-13, décembre 1967–mai 1968, 163–169.

Thériault, Norman. 2006. "Metropolis bleu." *Le Devoir* (Montréal), 25–26 mars, 2006, G1.

Tremblay, Michel. 1968. *Les belles-soeurs*. Montréal : Holt Rinehart et Winston: Théâtre vivant, 6.

_____. 1978. *La grosse femme d'à côté est enceinte*. Montréal: Leméac.

_____. 1980. *Thérèse et Pierrette à l'école des Saints-Anges*. Montréal: Leméac.

_____. 1982. *La Duchesse et le roturier*. Montréal: Leméac.

Urquhart, Jane, ed. 2009. *The Penguin Book of Canadian Short Stories*. Toronto: Penguin.

Weintraub, William. 1996. *City Unique: Montreal Days and Nights in the 40s and 50s*. Toronto: McClelland & Stewart.

_____. 2001. *Getting Started: A Memoir of the 50s*. Toronto: McClelland & Stewart.

Westley, Margaret. 1990. *Remembrance of Grandeur: The Anglo-Protestant Elite of Montreal, 1900-1950*. Montréal: Libre expression.

Whiteman, Bruce. 1994. *Lasting Impressions: A Short History of English Publishing in Quebec*. Montreal: Véhicule Press.

Williams, Raymond. 1985. *Culture and Society 1780–1950*. London: The Hogarth Press.

Yanofsky, Joel. 1992. "Field Notes — Hoping for the Best." *Books in Canada*, Jan–Feb. 1992, 8–9.

Index